Resingled: Survive and Then Thrive

Leverage Behavioral Science to Recover and Find Your Ideal Partner

By Laura Heft, Ph.D.

ReSingled: Survive and Then Thrive
Leverage Behavioral Science to Recover and Find Your Ideal Partner

Published by GrowOptimism
520 S. Brentwood
Clayton, MO 63105

ISBN: 978-1-955191-00-5

Cover design by Jim Saurbaugh, JS Graphic Design

publisher accept no responsibility for inaccuracies or omissions, and the author and publisher specifically disclaim any liability, loss, or risk, whether personal, financial, or otherwise, that is incurred as a consequence, directly or indirectly, from the use and/or application of any of the contents of this book.

Dedication

I want to start by thanking and acknowledging my ex-boyfriend for several things. First, for sharing himself and his life with me for two wonderful years. I greatly appreciated our time together and was very, very happy. I enjoyed doing simple things like raking the yard, getting ready for work in the morning, sitting on the back patio in the evenings, listening and discovering music together, as well as our great trips, adventures, and conversations. Second, for the inspiration and need to write this book, and third, the ReSingled title for this book (his idea).

I want to dedicate this book to the many people who have inspired me on my journey. Thank you Dr. Erin Shannon, who has not only been a great healer for me personally but also introduced me to so many fabulous healing tools and resources, and I consider to be a great friend. Thanks to the gurus who taught me and inspired me: Abraham Hicks, Martin Seligman, Wayne Dyer, David Feinstein, Donna Eden, Nick Ortner, Brad Yates, Cathy Kramer, and so many others too numerous to mention.

Finally, but not least important, my friends and family who gave me a home when I needed it and supported me through some dark times. My children (Monica, Susan, Adam, Becky, and Colin) and sisters (Karen, Julie, Lisa, Mary, and Sarah) were there for me, listened, went out with me, and encouraged me. Last, but not least, my close and supportive friends and soulmates: Jane, Jayne, Megan, Therese, Elaine, Shawn, Eric, and John.

Table of Contents

Table of Contents

Preface
Not Just Another Breakup Book

For most of my life I didn't understand how difficult a breakup could be or what it was like to go through it. I was married for 33 years and I didn't have a lot of experience with dating or breaking up. I knew people who went through breakups; I watched their suffering. I tried to be there for them as they went through the heartache, but I was naïve about how challenging a serious breakup could be or how excruciating the pain could be. That all changed when I went through a sudden and unexpected breakup that I didn't exactly choose. There were a number of reasons it was a tough breakup, but for me in particular, as an expert in the field of optimism, positive thinking, and behavior change, the breakup set me back in ways I never expected and didn't understand.

There were days when I felt intense sadness, anger, loneliness, and rejection. I am writing this book because I felt and saw so much totally unnecessary pain, suffering, hurt, and so many misunderstandings, assumptions, and mistakes, following dating and the end of relationships, that I felt compelled to change the way we handle relationships— both ending and beginning.

I decided to apply what I know about behavioral science and emotions (the head and the heart) to help me get through the challenge of an ended relationship. This book is designed to help you use the same behavioral science, tools, and awareness to recover from a breakup faster, and get the relationship you want next time around.

As I was writing this, I realized that there must be a lot of other good breakup books out there, but this book offers something different.

There are three things I want to offer you:

1) Leverage the science of the mind-body connection (the head and the heart) to
2) Survive a breakup in a healthy way, quickly
3) Position you to get the ideal relationship as soon as possible

I hope you'll find this book different than the myriad of self-help relationship books out there, and particularly helpful in a few ways. As someone who worked in the corporate world for 20+ years, I understand the value of getting to the point quickly and concisely. This book was written with that intention, so you'll get to the "meat" you need faster. Also because I am a psychologist and behavioral scientist the approaches in the book are backed with scientific research on what will help you create lasting change faster.

This book is organized into three sections. The first section focuses on surviving the breakup, Part 2 focuses on healing the emotions that torment us during and after a breakup, and the last part gives the path forward for your ideal relationship.

Each chapter includes a summary of key points, and if you are interested, there are resources (e.g., websites, books, etc.) provided by chapter at the end of the book. The resources are not intended to be an exhaustive representation of all the best resources, instead, they are provided to help you get started with topics you may be interested in.

You can approach this book a few different ways. Skim through the whole thing and then go back and read the parts that are most relevant. Read Part 1 thoroughly if you experienced a breakup in the last year (unless you made the decision to break up and therefore, it is possibly less painful). It is also worth noting that you might benefit from reading Part 1 if you still have strong feelings when you think about your ex. This could include positive feelings (e.g., longing, fantasizing, or love) or negative feelings (e.g., hate, anger, sadness, regret). If you have experienced many breakups in your life, you will also benefit from Part 1, but you should definitely spend some quality time in Part 2. Everyone should read Part 3! ***If you skip Part 1 or 2, be sure to read the chapters in Part 1 on Emotions and Your Busy Brain and Brain Biases. Understanding these concepts are foundational for making sense out of the rest of the book.***

Preface

Part 1: Surviving the Breakup

Understanding what the hell is happening. Why are breakups so ridiculously hard? Why am I still feeling so awful? How long is this going to last?

Breakups can be extremely challenging to say the least. Sometimes it takes a long time to get through them. The aftermath can be debilitating on many levels and the pain can be excruciating. ***The goal of this book is to help you move through the pain of the breakup quicker, in a healthier way, so you can get back to a normal state and into a better relationship the next time.*** Part one is intended to explain the science and psychology behind what happens after the breakup and provide ideas to help you heal faster and cope more effectively.

There are important reasons we ***need*** to understand what is happening. As humans we want to know why bad things happen to us; it helps give us a sense of control. Understanding the science behind the breakup may make some of the craziness a little more tolerable. Knowing that the pain you are going through is normal and a natural reaction for all human beings could help you feel better about your situation faster… and may provide some relief.

Secondly, when we understand what's happening, we can manage it better. When we are in the middle of something as highly emotionally charged as a breakup, we can lose perspective and may feel, do, or say things that are out of character and may cause lasting damage and regret. A friend once told me that people going through divorce are crazy for about a year. Some of the negative behaviors following a breakup might include retaliation, stalking, or serial dating/sex. You might even be a victim of these behaviors or perhaps the perpetrator, or both. These types of actions may also lead to embarrassment, regret, pain to family and friends, a bad reputation, futile attempts to replace your ex, and may even damage your opportunities with potential new partners who might have otherwise been a great fit. Perhaps you've experienced one or more of these issues of collateral damage.

Unfortunately, these types of behaviors are not helpful and often make things worse. On top of all the sadness and anger related to the loss of the relationship, the negative behavior can alienate you from the very people you need to help you heal. This leads to you feeling even worse about yourself and the situation. Understanding the "why" behind your thoughts, feelings, and actions may help you manage the situation, emotions, and curb the craziness.

Before we launch into the science and psychology behind the aftermath of a breakup, it's important to acknowledge that all breakups are not the same. Of course, there are different levels of severity and pain depending on the length of your relationship, the level of your commitment (e.g., casual dating vs. co-habitating vs. marriage), the nature of the breakup (e.g., annoying habits vs. unwillingness to commit vs. cheating), whether you or your partner made the decision to breakup, and your relationship history (e.g., the number and types of relationships and breakups you've had in the past), etc. All of these contingencies factor into how you interpret and respond to the breakup. Recognizing these huge differences, you'll need to pick and choose which aspects of the information provided in this book are most applicable to your situation. Think about it as a menu of choices. Pick the suggestions that fit for you and leave the rest. Let's start with some basics that are universally applicable.

Part 1: Surviving the Breakup

Chapter One:

Trauma

No matter what anyone else may say, breakups *are* a big deal. While you may not typically think of trauma as a word that describes a breakup, in most cases, the end of a meaningful relationship is traumatic. What you are feeling is a meaningful loss and you must go through the mourning phase. There are a couple of analogies to help you think about the seriousness of the damage done and the critical need to take care of yourself with extreme kindness, compassion, and tender loving care (TLC). The first relates to a physical injury and the second relates to death.

Physical Injury – Broken Heart

Coping with the loss of a relationship is one of life's biggest challenges. The loss of the relationship creates an emotional wound—*it's called a broken heart for a reason!* In some ways, it could be comparable to a physical injury like a broken leg. After breaking a leg, we can't go about our lives as if nothing has happened; the bones need time to heal and so do broken hearts. We need to think about the seriousness of the emotional wound in a very similar way. There must be treatment, time for healing, and recovery. That's really what this book is about. It's a way to guide you through those necessary steps and then find the relationship you want and deserve.

Loss and Grief

While the loss of a relationship is obviously not the same as the loss experienced when a loved one dies, there are similarities. Grief is described as the emotional suffering a person feels when someone they loved is no longer in their life. Often, the pain of loss can feel overwhelming.

A person grieving may experience all kinds of difficult and unexpected emotions. It can even disrupt their physical health, make it difficult to sleep, eat, or even think straight. These are normal reactions to loss—and the more significant the loss, the more intense the grief will be. The loss from a breakup is also very real, and people ending a relationship will likely experience grief.

The 5 Stages of Grief was a model (Kübler-Ross, E.,1970) developed to describe the grieving process related to death, but provides a useful framework for understanding any significant loss. While the grieving process is very individual and there is not a right or wrong response to loss, the model is useful in helping people understand some of the normal emotions they may experience. The five stages of grief are:

Denial: "This can't be happening to me."

Anger: "*Why* is this happening? Who is to blame?"

Bargaining: "Please make this stop. Fix it and in return I will _____."

Depression: "My life is ruined. I'm too sad to do anything."

Acceptance: "I'm at peace with what happened. Everything happens for a reason and this will work out in the end."

The Kubler-Ross 5 Stages of Grief consists of levels or stages of emotions which are experienced by a person who is approaching death or is a survivor of the death of a loved one.

Not everyone who grieves goes through all of these stages in the same order or at all. In fact, the grieving process can be quite a roller coaster. Some days are up and some are down. You may even be up and down in the same day, multiple times, hitting more than one stage or going backward. The ride is usually rougher in the beginning, and the lows may be deep and long. You may proceed through most of the stages, only to find yourself back in denial the next day. The process is uncomfortable and difficult to go through. It may seem like it is out of your control; you may feel at the mercy of your feelings, fearing the experience of more negative emotions each morning when you wake up.

> *"Grief is like the ocean; it comes on waves ebbing and flowing. Sometimes the water is calm, and sometimes it is overwhelming. All we can do is learn to swim."*
>
> *Vicki Harrison*

Unfortunately, there is also no timetable associated with the grieving process. Eventually the rougher times should be less painful, as well as fewer and further between, but it takes time to work through a loss.

Relationships Meet a Lot of Basic Human Needs

Great relationships are *awesome*, which is why we feel such a loss when they end! They meet a lot of our basic human needs, which is why many people long to find great partners and live in committed relationships. When the relationship is over, many of the important needs that were previously satisfied (or at least seemingly satisfied) by the relationship are no longer met, and that results in a critical gap in our lives.

Let's start with some basic psychology to explain how that works.

 Abraham Maslow (1954) identified five critical needs people strive to meet to be happy. Here is the typical pyramid that depicts Maslow's Hierarchy of Needs:

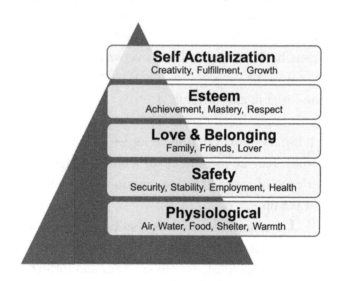

Very simply and starting at the bottom, a person must fulfill the need at that level before they can move upward. For example, until your physiological needs are met, you will not be able to concern yourself with safety and security. If your needs for safety and security are unmet, you will not be able to pursue love and belonging... and without that, self-esteem is out the window.

The most obvious need threatened by a breakup is the *need for belonging and love*. However, breakups also likely impact other needs too. For example, esteem needs can be triggered by feelings of rejection, regret, or unworthiness. For many people, the end of the relationship can also mean that safety/security needs are challenged. This can occur when people are married, living together, believe they have a future together, or are financially dependent on the other, and the breakup means their homes and/or financial stability changes. Let's take a deeper dive into each one.

Belonging and Love

We all need to feel loved and accepted. Being loved is not just a "nice to have" emotional need. Humans are hardwired to make connections with others in order to live a healthy, fulfilling life. Loving and being loved are basic human needs, almost as vital as our physiological need for air, food, and water, followed quickly by our need for safety and security.

Relationships with friends, family, coworkers, religious groups, sports teams, and other kinds of groups play an important role in fulfilling this human need. Most people also long for a deeper, more intimate connection with another person through a romantic relationship.

In romantic relationships, partners are often tasked with satisfying the lion's share of the need for belonging and love. This is the person with whom you have regular communication ranging from the daily "how was your day" to the more intimate sharing of personal hopes, dreams, and fears, as well as everything in between. Your partner is someone you want to spend time with, share meals, hobbies, and maybe religious beliefs and practices. They are a trusted friend, the person who has your back when you're in trouble, and satisfies your need for human touch/sex, etc. Depending on the relationship, you may list them as your "who to contact in case of emergency," they go with you to family functions, are your travel companion, and your "+1" for social events. Many partners live together and make commitments to each other, and this person might be considered your "family."

Herein lies a major challenge with a breakup. Since we depend so heavily on our romantic partner, it can be devastating to lose the person who is your best friend, the one you talk with every day, sleep with, and who fills your events calendar, etc. So many aspects are blown up at the same time. Breakups leave us with not only a huge love deficit, but simultaneously with an intense loneliness and longing for our best friend, confidant, and dinner companion—all rolled up into one person. With the breakup, you fall down at least one rung in Maslow's pyramid, and many times several. Increased vulnerability occurs with every downward step.

One further complication here is related to the other people involved with the relationship. For example, a couple who has children together can end their romantic relationship, but obviously they don't stop being parents together and need to maintain some form of a relationship for the children. After a breakup, partners may be feeling particularly vulnerable due to the love loss and could become fearful about the loss of the children's love too. This can lead to destructive feelings and behaviors such as competing for the children's affections or sabotaging the other partner's relationship with the children. Other challenges include common friends and other family members. Following the breakup, who gets "custody" of the friends or extended family members? This is particularly important because both partners will likely need these relationships for support. The potential collateral damage is staggering.

Esteem

Self-esteem refers to a person's sense of self-respect or self-worth; it describes how much you appreciate or like yourself. The idea here is that your value comes just from being who you are, you don't have to do a thing to earn it. It doesn't matter what you've accomplished, how many failed relationships you've been in, how much money you have, or really anything that comes from outside of you. Your self-esteem is purely a factor of your internal value. However, most people base their self-esteem on external accomplishments.

Following a breakup, it is very natural to try to figure out what happened. You struggle hard to understand and make sense of the breakup so you can mitigate the pain and avoid it happening again. It is normal and healthy to question the things you said or did that contributed to damaging the relationship and take responsibility for those things.

In reality, I can't think of any situations in which both people aren't partially responsible in some way for the breakup. In addition, the relationship *failed* (regardless of what happened or who is at fault) and both parties own the collapse to some extent. This failure can shake your self-esteem to the core as you may naturally doubt or blame yourself. Even a person who feels blameless about the relationship ending may still chastise him/herself for making a bad choice of partner in the first place, not seeing a problem quickly enough, or investing so much time and energy with the wrong person.

If a person accepts all the blame for the relationship ending or alternatively, none of the blame for their part in the breakup, either extreme can damage self-esteem. The former may result in an overly severe attack on self-esteem and the latter attempts to protect an already fragile sense of self-esteem with a false sense of arrogance. Neither of these is helpful in learning from the experience and growing. Alternatively, taking responsibility for your *part* in the relationship ending is a more balanced approach that can help you process the relationship while maintaining a healthy level of self-esteem.

When a relationship ends because one person wants to move on, the other person will likely feel a strong sense of *rejection,* which, as a result, can also wound self-esteem. In this case, even the most confident person might ask, "Why don't they like me?" Or "What's wrong with me?"

Other more subtle challenges to self-esteem may also be present following breakups. For example, did you "lose" yourself in the relationship and no longer know who you are, what you want, or like who you have become? Sometimes individuals lose their identities in the context of becoming a couple. One or both of the partners may have become so enmeshed in the other person, they no longer acted or thought of themselves as individuals. Alternatively, were there compromises you made in terms of what is important to you that you no longer like or want? While the process of rediscovering you and who you want to be is healthy, it is another level of instability you may be dealing with when a relationship ends.

Finally, a word about ghosting. When the reason for the relationship ending is ambiguous or suspicious (e.g., someone "ghosts" or withdraws/blocks communication from the other person), it is natural to question why and what happened. When answers are not apparent, it is very human to want to understand. However, the pursuit of a "reason" can make you crazy. A natural conclusion in these situations is that we did something wrong or we were unacceptable in some way. However, when a person leaves a relationship through ghosting, they likely have their own emotional problems. This is not a reflection of you. If this type of withdrawal behavior was a pattern in your relationship, you may need additional support to manage the longer-term impact on you.

Safety and Physiological Needs

The stress associated with a breakup could be so debilitating it could limit a person's ability to focus and function effectively at work, therefore threatening their safety needs. When the couple has been living together, the insecurity of losing their home may also result in a high level of anxiety (e.g., where am I going to live... and in the immediate days after the breakup, where are my clothes, my medications, how do I shop/cook/eat, etc.?). In the worst case, if a partner was financially dependent on their ex, and/or will struggle to support themselves (and maybe their children) alone, it can be devastating.

Any of these situations could challenge your safety and physiological needs, effectively taking you back down to the very base of the pyramid. At those levels your sense of survival may kick in and lead to some desperate thinking and behavior.

Maslow's theory asserts that people advance up the pyramid only after the needs at the lower levels are met. In other words, a person worried about where their next meal is coming from can't operate at the relationship or self-esteem levels. So someone who was enjoying life at the highest levels of the pyramid can quickly fall back down to the bottom without a safety net following a breakup.

Dealing with unmet needs at *multiple* levels of the pyramid is more complicated and much more difficult to deal with. The greater number of needs that are unmet the more complex the healing process and the longer it takes to recover. A person dealing with a housing change, financial or job instability cannot deal with relationship or self-esteem needs until their physiological/safety needs are resolved. So, if this is the case with your breakup, your healing process will likely take longer than that of a person who did not fall as far down on the pyramid.

*The impact of falling down multiple levels of the pyramid at once was a new awareness for me as I experienced it firsthand. While I would describe myself as generally a fairly high functioning person (e.g., good job, stable family, healthy lifestyle), able to support myself financially, and maybe even operating at the self-actualization apex of the pyramid, my last breakup totally devastated me. I **loved** my ex-boyfriend and was living with him in his home while my condo was being renovated. The breakup was totally unexpected, came from out of the blue, and I was unprepared.*

I found myself with a one-hour window to vacate what I thought of as my home at 9:00 p.m. on a Sunday night, with nowhere to go and having to work the next day. This happened three weeks before Christmas. On top of everything else, my children and grandchildren were traveling to be with us for the holiday and were scheduled to stay at his home. My heart was broken, but I could hardly even deal with the relationship loss because I was in survival mode. I dropped all the way down Maslow's pyramid to the safety/security level. I spent my time looking for places to stay, (investigating hotels, Airbnb rentals, apartments, friends' and family houses), moving from place to place, living out of multiple suitcases, trying to find and keep track of my belongings that were stored in four different locations.

I went through all of this with an incredibly heavy heart. I missed him desperately, but I was also angry at him for doing this to us. Each day I had to pull it together to get to work and somehow fake it through the day, not to mention figuring out where I would stay the next day/week/month. My condo renovation added extra pressure with delays, cost

21

overruns, permitting issues, all of which were preventing me from having a home to which to return. I did not cope well with this on top of the pain of losing my best friend and lover. It set me in quite a tailspin. I remembered observing that people who lived together as a couple and then broke up were in a very bad situation. I also thought that the difficulties related to finding a new place to live might keep a couple together longer than they should be. However, what I couldn't see from the outside was the level of difficulty that resulted from the simultaneous disruption of so many critical areas of life all at once – until I experienced it for myself.

I'm certain that my needs at every level of the pyramid were threatened to some degree. Dropping all the way down to my safety and security needs made the breakup more traumatic and therefore required more recovery time.

This chapter was intended to help you understand why breakups are so hard. Rushing through the grieving process, distracting yourself from the pain, and avoiding your emotions will almost guarantee you'll be in the same situation down the road. The hope here is that knowing the science behind why it's so hard might help you be more patient and kinder to yourself, which will actually speed your recovery and better prepare you to get the ideal partner.

Getting It Right

- As humans, when bad things happen, we want to better understand the reason. It provides a sense of control. This section provided some of the rationale and science behind the pain of a breakup in the hope of making the situation a little more tolerable.

- Breakups involve real trauma and create a real emotional wound similar to physical injuries. The pain of a broken heart is real, and needs time and TLC to heal.
- The end of a relationship is a loss. Understanding the five stages of grief (denial, anger, bargaining, depression, and acceptance) may help you make sense of your experience in the breakup aftermath.
- Maslow's Hierarchy of Needs helps explain the multiple important needs that may go unmet when a relationship ends. At a minimum, there's a deficit in the need for belonging and love. Self-esteem may also be challenged from a sense of rejection or failure of the relationship. Depending on the length of the relationship and commitment (e.g., marriage, financial support, co-habitating), even the need for safety may be jeopardized.
- The more core needs (e.g., love, esteem, safety) that are under attack, the more difficult the recovery from the breakup.
- Rushing through the grieving process, distracting yourself from the pain, and avoiding your emotions will almost guarantee you'll repeat the same relationship pattern again.
- Understanding that the pain and sadness is normal may encourage you to give yourself permission to work through the grief in a more effective way and get the ideal relationship you desire.

Trauma

Chapter Two:

Emotions and Your Busy Brain

Emotions can be simply described as your feelings (e.g., happiness, fear, anger, boredom, frustration). Everyone experiences emotions, but they are more important than many people realize. They are a key factor in helping you survive and thrive in life. For example, fear protects you from danger, feeling playful or silly helps you cope with stress, and love helps you connect to your "tribe" (the people who care for you and help protect you). Scientists debate the definition of emotions, how they are measured, what triggers them, and how they are expressed. Emotions are a complex state that results in both psychological and physical changes, thus a mind-body connection.

While you are probably familiar with the idea of emotions having a psychological effect, you may be surprised to learn about the physiological side of emotions. However, consider how a child who is afraid to go to school may complain of an upset stomach, or an adult experiencing a problem at work may notice symptoms of anxiety such as tension in their neck or shoulders, rapid breathing, or increased heart rate.

The research on understanding emotions is still in the relatively early stages of development. Learning about what triggers your emotional reactions, becoming aware of those reactions, and responding to your feelings in a healthy way is very important to your future relationship success. It will also be important to recognize the huge cost of avoiding or suppressing your feelings. The second part of the book is dedicated to providing a better understanding of emotions and helping you learn to manage them better. However, this section of the book will help you begin to better understand the impact of your emotions and highlight some of the many feelings that may be associated with your breakup.

Negative Emotions

Wow. No way around it. There is simply a lot of emotional pain and negative emotion associated with the end of a relationship. For the reasons already described, it can be debilitating. The anger, sadness, hurt, and despair that follow can be overwhelming—piled on top of the challenge of dealing with change. It's no wonder there are so many songs written about breakups.

The emotional pain and trauma are not the only problem. When we have strong (negative) emotional reactions, we struggle to process information clearly and rationally. Negative emotions seem to hijack our brains.

 Emotions powerfully and predictably influence and often degrade decision making with unwanted results – this occurs without our conscious awareness (Lerner, et al., 2015).

Once the fear, anger, hurt, or resentment enter into the picture, we tend to shut down. In conversations, it's as if our ears stop working. We miss information that is shared, only selectively hear what matches our emotions and beliefs, and disregard other information. In many cases, we can't hear what the other person is saying or accurately determine what they meant. Errors in perception and judgment can occur regularly under normal conditions, but when we experience highly charged emotions, it is especially difficult to process information rationally, so our judgment and decision-making abilities are temporarily impaired.

One set of negative emotions you will likely experience after a breakup is related to change. For many, many people, "change" raises a lot of negative feelings (e.g., dread, discomfort, fear, avoidance). In a breakup you experience *a lot of change* related to the loss of your partner. You may lose your best friend, your "go-to" person for daily communication, the person you eat meals with, and maybe even who you live with. The more your lives were woven together (e.g., in the case of marriage or co-habitation), the more disruption you encounter when the relationship ends. In these cases, even the most basic things you have been taking for granted change.

For example, in addition to thinking, "What am I going to do on the weekend now and with whom," I may also be dealing with, "How do I eat meals alone and cook for one? Who do I tell what happened at work today or what the kids did?" You might be tackling big issues like where and how you want to live (e.g., house, condo, or apartment, with a roommate or alone?). You may be thinking, "Which of our shared friends are still mine, how will I handle a holiday or take vacation?" So much change in so many aspects of our life can be overwhelming.

As humans, we are not comfortable with change or ambiguity. Some people fight change more than others, but we all resist it to some extent – it's an evolutionary instinct to protect ourselves from the unknown. It's worth acknowledging that some of the negative emotions you are feeling are not completely related to the loss of your romantic partner. A portion of the turmoil is likely related to the changes that happened as the result of the breakup. In addition to dealing with a broken heart, the end of the relationship means you lose the normality of your life, your routines, many of your plans, and your safety net.

Separating this out can help you put the pain in perspective. Attributing some of your pain to the change process may help minimize the distress associated with the situation. Since we've all been through a lot of change in life, and understand that it is only temporarily uncomfortable, we can have faith that we'll survive and get through it okay eventually. After all, you have a lot of history surviving change. Be confident that you will look back on this and not feel the loss as intensely at some point.

Our Busy Brains

As if dealing with negative emotions weren't enough of a challenge in coping with a breakup, the challenge of cognitive biases piles on as well. A report from University of California, San Diego (Bohn & Short, 2012) suggests the average American consumes 34 gigabytes of content and 100,000 words of information in a single day. This doesn't mean we read 100,000 words a day — it means that 100,000 words cross our eyes and ears in a day through television, radio, internet, text messages, and video games. This is just the external information. Your brain also gets information from your body (e.g., it's cold, I have a headache, or it's time to eat again) and your thoughts (I miss my ex, my boss was rude to me, or I need to schedule my next vacation). Our conscious minds can only handle a tiny fraction of this information, so our brains take cognitive shortcuts to help sort the most relevant information and filter out the rest. Otherwise, we would be totally overwhelmed and incapacitated by the prospect of evaluating the tsunami of stimuli we are confronted with every day.

This all happens automatically without our awareness. Our brains are programmed to do this sorting and sifting work on autopilot, so we can focus on other things that take more attention and conscious thought. Our brains do a wonderful job freeing us up to think about and do more important things. That behind-the-scenes work our brain does helps us function in the world. But who programs the brain to decide what gets through the filter and what gets blocked? You do. Your education, upbringing, beliefs, thoughts, and prior experiences train your brain to prioritize and pick out what is most relevant – most of it happens without your conscious awareness.

These shortcuts are also known as cognitive biases. These biases filter what gets registered in your mind and what gets ignored. Your pre-programmed shortcuts are operating behind the scenes all day, every day, making choices about what you notice and what you ***don't*** notice. While this is a wonderful function that helps us survive, it can also lead to unconscious or implicit bias.

Unconsicous or implicit bias is when people have attitudes or make stereotypical judgements about people or things without conscious awareness.

These biases have serious consequences for how we perceive, talk with, and act toward other people. In the next chapter, we'll look at several of the most powerful and harmful biases that may play out in a breakup. We'll refer to these several times in the book and will add others as we progress through the chapters.

The good news is that there are ways to overcome these biases. Becoming aware that they exist is an important first step. This awareness can help you start to spot them in your thinking and decision making. Next you can challenge yourself to consider alternative explanations, contrary evidence, and other options vs. landing on the first thing that comes into your mind. Finally, you can set up some safety nets to keep you from falling into the trap of your biases. For example, you can set up a habit of waiting a day before making big decisions to ensure your emotions aren't overly influencing your decision. You'll learn more about these strategies in the upcoming chapters.

Getting It Right

- Emotions play a critical role in our relationships and their endings. Learning what triggers emotions, how we react and respond to those emotions in a healthy way is very important to future relationship success.

- Your brain is bombarded by far more information that you can process. The result is your brain taking cognitive shortcuts behind the scenes to sort and prioritize the most relevant information and filter out the rest.

- You actually "program" your brain by what you focus on. These shortcuts, although helpful in general, are called biases because without complete information, they often lead to false perceptions. Unfortunately, we operate in life under many biases, often with serious consequences.

- The good news is that you can overcome these biases. Awareness helps you spot them in your thinking and decision making so you can take steps to reduce any unwanted outcomes.

Chapter Three

Brain Biases

There are many biases that impact us in numerous ways, including in our relationships. Have you ever been in an upsetting conversation in which your partner swears they said something, and you swear they didn't? This is sometimes jokingly referred to as selective hearing—people hear what they want to hear. But the science of cognitive biases suggests that this is not an intentional decision to ignore (or not remember) what was said. The truth is you may have both been right. The stress or pain of the situation may have impaired your ability to hear or process the information (cognitive overload) or your cognitive biases *filtered out* the information. This oversight was not done on purpose, but it's really an important consideration in understanding relationships, misunderstandings, and what we need to do to overcome harmful biases. The next sections explain how this happens.

The Power of Negativity

As humans, we are automatically programmed to focus on negative information. Unfortunately, bad news usually gets more attention than good news; this is one of the most menacing threats to successful relationships and our happiness in general. Have you ever noticed how we ruminate on an insult but brush off a compliment? We are drawn to look at car accidents as we drive by; we are mesmerized by the news following a disaster; and mistakes made by public officials or celebrities always hit the front page. News stations, gossip magazines, and political campaigns understand this negativity bias very well and use it to sell. Bad news gets more of our attention because of the negativity bias. Unfortunately, when negative information is given more weight, it often leads to errors in judgment.

 The negativity bias, is the idea that things of a more negative nature (e.g. unpleasant thoughts, emotions, or social interactions; harmful/traumatic events) get more attention and have a greater effect on one's psychological state and processes than neutral or positive things (even when the intensity is about the same).

Negative thinking and experiences grab our attention, stick in our memories, and influence the decisions that we make. Consider the case of something most of us are familiar with—online product reviews. Research shows that there are a lot more positive reviews than negative (Fowler & De Avila, 2009), but they are seen as less helpful (Herr et al., 1991) and therefore have a weaker effect on purchase decisions than negative reviews (Basuroy et al., 2003; Chevalier & Mayzlin, 2006).

It is very important to understand this because the negativity bias has a powerful personal impact on our relationships as well. For example, you may meet a perfectly nice person online and have a great phone conversation to get to know them better. While you've been having positive communications for a couple of weeks and the call is going great for 30 minutes, at the first sign of something you don't like, you could change your whole attitude toward that person (often without confirming your impression). So after 29 minutes of great conversation suggesting that this person could be a great partner, one bit of data (regardless of how vague) could rule them out. This may seem like an exaggeration, but the negativity bias is very powerful. It's worth your time to observe whether and how it plays out in your life.

It's difficult to move forward after negative experiences because they weigh so heavily in our thinking. In most cases, past pains and traumas have a very long tail. They stand out in our memories more vividly and therefore continue to plague us well into the future! Here are some of the costs of the negativity bias in terms of relationships.

Take for example someone who complains about the fact that "all my relationships end badly." Perhaps you were in a great relationship that was fun-filled and exciting for two years, but you can't remember the good because you are stuck in the pain of the breakup. Because the pain is most prominent (we naturally focus on the negative), you can't keep the totality of the relationship (including the substantially good aspects) in perspective. This emphasis on the pain may limit your willingness to risk dating again.

What are your thoughts about your opportunities to have a great relationship? Because of negativity bias, you are more likely to focus on pessimistic thoughts and fears than positive ones... which means you are probably more negative than positive about your prospects. Even if you have some positive thoughts, there are likely some negative thoughts that end up being stronger and therefore overwhelm your positive thoughts, effectively cancelling them out or never allowing them to "make the front page."

Fight or Flight

Our tendency to pay more attention to bad things and overlook good things is likely a result of evolution. People were more likely to survive if they paid more attention to negative information because there were bigger consequences than if they didn't (Baumeister et al., 2001). Our ancestors had to scan the environment for danger and threats as a matter of life or death (e.g., predator approaching). When danger was detected, the body reacted with a series of physiological changes designed to prepare for a fight or a "flight" to escape.

For example, a high conflict situation can trigger your heart to pound, muscles to tense, blood to flow away from extremities, and the breath to quicken—all physiological reactions to prepare for fight or flight. Focused attention on dangers kept people alive in the past.

Fight or flight: the instinctive sequence of hormonal and physiological responses to a threatening situation, which readies one either to resist forcibly or to run away.

Understanding the Stress Response, Harvard Health Publishing (2020)

Although today those same types of physical threats don't exist as much, the brain continues to scan for and focus on the negative as a way of keeping us safe. The fight-flight response to danger in the environment is also triggered by threats of potential emotional "dangers." Your brain and body don't differentiate between physical and emotional stimuli. When we feel threatened by a partner's anger, accusations, an ultimatum, or maybe even simple verbal insults, we may perceive the words as a personal attack that can put us in fight-flight mode. Again, our brains are looking for danger, so the negativity bias is stacked against us.

Another important point about how the fight-flight response impacts a relationship is related to how the body operates when the fight-flight response is activated. In these situations, our ability to objectively perceive information, listen clearly, and process information effectively may be impaired due to the prioritization and mobilization of the body's most critical resources for the fight-flight response. Your brain is taking a shortcut to "survival" and weeding out everything else, even what's important to your ability to properly assess the situation.

At the beginning of the chapter, we described a situation in which one person swore they didn't hear something the other person swore they said. The fight-flight response was most likely the culprit. In the stressful situation, the person sending the message may have intended to say something but got distracted, or they actually shared it, but the other person was too stressed to hear it because their body was shifting resources for protection.

As a side note, this physiological response to emotional "threats" that are as simple as an argument over whose turn it is to cook dinner is essentially an overreaction by the body—it is not at risk of being harmed. Over time, this repeated activation of the stress response takes an unhealthy toll on the body.

Confirmation Bias

As we've just discussed, as humans we notice more negative information and react more strongly to it. Now enter the confirmation bias which essentially multiplies the negativity effect. Due to the confirmation bias, your mind searches for information to confirm your beliefs, thoughts, and perceptions, and disregards information that doesn't support them. This all happens subconsciously, without your awareness.

Confirmation bias: the tendency to actively seek supporting evidence (and give it more weight) as confirmation of one's existing beliefs while ignoring opposing information.

It's very important to understand the confirmation bias. The workplace example below demonstrates how it works.

For example, consider a manager interviewing two candidates to fill a job. The job is being filled because the person who had the job last got pregnant, had a baby, went on leave, and then quit. The manager, frustrated by covering for the employee during the maternity leave and now having to hire someone, doesn't want to take a chance of repeating the situation again. When the two female candidates arrive, the manager notices that candidate A appears to be of child-bearing age and candidate B is much older, and in fact mentions that she is a grandmother. The manager, fearful of hiring another woman who will get pregnant, forms a belief that candidate B will be a better fit for the job.

During the interview with candidate A, the manager unconsciously looks for information that confirms that she is not a fit. Sure enough, several "warning flags" come up and her stellar track record is minimized. Alternatively, in the interview with candidate B, several relevant concerns were overlooked (e.g., the fact that she was not familiar with some of the software systems used and made several communication mistakes). This is an example of the confirmation bias. The well-intentioned manager was likely not even aware of how the bias influenced the hiring decision, nor how unfair it was to the candidates.

The confirmation bias has significant implications for dating and relationships. It exacerbates the problem with the negativity bias. The combination of these biases prevents us from making a fair balanced evaluation of the facts on both sides of the story.

Of course, this is happening automatically without your conscious awareness. With the confirmation bias in play, what you focus on expands because it is what we see and experience; it's all our filter allows in. We focus on what we already *believe* to be true and that is then repeatedly reinforced. We need to retrain our brains in order to more effectively evaluate considering both positive and negative information.

Here is how this might play out in a relationship. Let's say you are interested in finding your ideal partner to start a long-term relationship. It seems likely that you would be excited and thinking good thoughts about the possibility of a great relationship. For example, you might be thinking,

"I'm so excited about my next relationship. It is going to feel so good to find someone to spend my life with, someone who knows and understands me." However, since you aren't in a relationship now, you may also be somewhat focused on the gap between what you want but don't have (whether you are actively aware of it or not). Therefore, you may also be thinking, "I'm so tired of being alone and I want to find my soulmate—my ideal partner now." You may hardly be conscious of this subtle thought, but here's where those cognitive biases come into play.

The negativity bias puts more emphasis on the subtle negative thought about **not** having the relationship you want than on the expectation you'll get into a great relationship. In addition, you may have had some bad relationship experiences in the past, so it's easy for more doubts to creep in. Then you may also have some body image issues (e.g., I'm not attractive because I've put on an extra 10 lbs.). So now we are layering on additional negative thoughts around the idea of finding a relationship.

Hopefully, you are seeing that the deck can easily be stacked on the negative side of the equation. So, who are the partners your brain is going to focus on? People who will prove you are correct. Through confirmation bias, your brain is filtering out the good prospects you desire, and instead seeing the potential partners you don't want. As crazy as it seems, you will find yourself meeting and attracted to potential partners who can't commit or will judge you for your appearance—ones who prove you can only get into a bad relationship or are not attractive enough to find a great partner… thus confirming your negative expectation.

Overconfidence Bias

One final bias worth mentioning in this section (more will be introduced in subsequent chapters) is called the overconfidence bias. It is fairly straightforward, and highlights the tendency to be overconfident in our abilities and decisions. For example, one research study asked participants to rate their driving skills. In a typical sample of the population, you would expect *most* people to be average and only a *small proportion* to be above and below average (i.e., normal distribution curve). However, this research found that almost 80% of participants thought they were above-average drivers (McCormick, et al., 1986). By definition, it is impossible for the majority of drivers to be above average. Clearly, these drivers were biased about their own driving abilities. This bias extends well beyond driving abilities. The same effect has been shown to occur in self-ratings of job and academic performance, estimates of IQ, healthy behaviors, memory, and even of our own popularity.

Overconfidence bias is the tendency to overestimate our abilities and talent. We mistakenly believe that we are better than we actually are.

The tendency to be overconfident doesn't necessarily mean that you are arrogant, but rather we all like to think the best of ourselves and don't like to think we aren't as good as others. The point of introducing the overconfidence bias is not to challenge your skills or talents. What's relevant here is to remember that we are all subject to errors in judgment from biases.

Being overconfident in your abilities could be a blind spot in many areas of your life, including your relationships. For example, are you overconfident in your ability to evaluate the compatibility of your potential partners? Are you a little too sure that your ex is totally responsible for the breakup and you did nothing wrong? Are you sure that most potential partners are only interested in you for your money or for sex? Are there really a very small number of partners in the world who could make you happy? Are you sure no partners would be interested in someone with three small children or who is overweight or has a "crappy" job? Hopefully the evidence regarding overconfidence will make it feel safe to reevaluate some of the thoughts and judgments you have been making that may be leading you down the wrong path.

A final note on overconfidence is the idea that since you now know how it can work against you, can you instead leverage it to help you? Are there areas of your life where you want to be more confident? For example, if you want to be more confident that you are attractive, interesting, and a real catch, try looking for the evidence to prove you are right and ignore or discount information that suggests you aren't.

Overcoming Biases

If you want to get the relationship you want, it will help to be willing and open to challenge your thinking. To start to move forward, we have to find ways to combat these brain biases. You will need to take additional steps to rewire your brain and challenge the automatic conclusions. Below are some steps you help you move in that direction:

1) Awareness: Be aware of these biases that influence your thinking and decisions. Begin to spot them so you can slow the automatic processes.

2) Pause: Scan to find out if you have any negative emotions that could be impacting your perceptions or decisions. If you find there are, wait for your emotions to calm, so you can more effectively evaluate your choices.

3) Seek Truth: Test your assumptions.

- Ask questions to confirm your judgments.
- Look for:
  o Alternative explanations – why else could this have happened?
  o Contrary evidence – is there any information that this could be wrong (remember the brain filters out evidence that doesn't support our position)?
  o Consider other options when you are making decisions – what alternative options are available?
- Broaden your perspective; ask trusted friends and family members (who aren't afraid to tell you the truth) to help you evaluate your situation.
- Safety Nets: If you want to avoid biases, what can you do to help you overcome them (e.g., wait a day before making important decisions or sending confrontational emails)?

Getting It Right

- Our brains are very busy and bombarded daily with far more stimuli than we can consider. The result: we develop biases that filter what needs attention and what can be ignored. These biases serve a very important purpose to help us focus and sift through an overwhelming amount of data. However, many of these shortcuts can be detrimental.

- One of the most powerful and destructive biases is the negativity bias. In an effort to protect us, our brains scan for more negative information so we can avoid injury. Therefore, negative information gets more attention and more weight. The harmful effect of this bias can extend to relationships too.

- The brain (and subsequently your body) reacts to stressful situations with the fight-flight reaction triggering a physiological response to protect the body. When the brain shifts the body into protective mode, it also impairs our judgment and decision-making capabilities. This occurs whether or not a situation is actually life-threatening.

- This fight-flight reaction responds to emotional stimuli as well. Your brain doesn't differentiate between the physical and emotional threats.

- The second most important bias related to relationships is the confirmation bias. Your brain searches only for information that "confirms" your beliefs and disregards anything that doesn't.

- Add insult to injury by activating the overconfidence bias that sets us up to believe we may be better than we really are, which can also be problematic for relationships.
- The good news is you can rewire your brain and overcome these biases! Humbly challenge your beliefs, thinking, and decisions. You can do this by becoming more aware, pausing before taking action, more intentionally seeking truth, and setting up safety nets.

Brain Biases

Chapter Four:

Let It Go... or Try Again?

Following a breakup, many people have to face a critical decision: try to get back together and make the relationship work or let it go. A further complication is that either you or your partner may want to give the relationship another try, but one of you does not.

There are a lot of good reasons to try to salvage the relationship. You found love with this person at some point, which is pretty special. You may still care for each other, you have an identity as a couple, a history together and might even have a family. You thought enough of this person to build a life together. This option may seem logical and more attractive because it also stops the immediate pain of the breakup. If you were happy at some point in the relationship, there's the possibility you will be happy again, right? People who go this route can at least say they did everything possible to try to save the relationship.

Basically, the decision comes down to whether you should make an additional investment of time, energy, and love in a relationship that didn't work before, or invest in something new that may or may not be better and is completely unknown. Maintaining the status quo of "the devil we know" (i.e., our broken relationship) may seem better than "the devil we don't know" (i.e., unknown potential opportunity of a new relationship). It is a difficult choice with no easy answer.

However, getting back together will also require work to fix whatever problem (or problems as there is usually more than one) caused the breakup, and the problems may not be fixable (if either or both parties are unwilling or unable to change). Trust must be rebuilt, and it is very fragile. Once lost, trust is extremely hard to regain (if at all), but it is not impossible if a decision is made to trust again.

If the issues that caused the breakup are not successfully addressed and changed, the same outcome is likely to happen again. If this is the case, it seems logical that you'll have to go through the pain again, and maybe with even greater pain now because you've invested more time, energy, and love. The price tag and potential pain at the end of the relationship just got higher. You may be setting yourself up for a sort of relationship posttraumatic stress disorder (PTSD).

Clearly, this is an important decision. Your future happiness depends on making the right choice. It should be made with the utmost care using your best logic. However, the odds are actually stacked against you in making this decision. Your ordinarily strong decision processes can be flawed because of some very human tendencies and those brain biases nudging you toward salvaging the relationship instead of moving forward with a new one. You need to be aware of these influences and understand what you can do about them to make a healthier and more optimal decision.

Let's look at three important considerations: 1) the impact of your emotions, 2) the need for changes to occur in order for the relationship to work, and 3) the cognitive biases that stack the deck.

Emotions

Following a breakup, you are in emotional pain. We don't need to go into more detail here; you know it and are living it! Getting back together looks like a way to eliminate the pain. Unfortunately, this complex decision to stay or go needs to be made at a time when you are under emotional duress and therefore operating without your best rational decision making. As you'll recall from the previous chapters, heightened emotions and decision making are never a good mix and limit your regularly strong capabilities in this area. Negative emotions and pain hijack our brains.

First, do not feel the need to rush into a decision. If you have broken up, the big decision to end the relationship has already been made. As much as possible, postpone the decision to reunite until your emotions are less intense. A simple test to determine if your emotions are influencing your decision is to check in and see if you have any anxiety, defensiveness, or any other emotion when you think about it. If you sense any emotions, they are influencing your decision.

In addition, if you are feeling pressure to make a decision because of:

- finances,
- your ex wants to get back together,
- you are afraid your ex is dating,
- you are afraid you made a mistake and are missing your chance to have a great relationship with your ex and/or,
- any other reason...

... stop and take a breath.

Be aware that these reasons are creating additional fear and stress, which further deteriorate your capacity to make a good decision! Take the time you need.

Also reach out to trusted friends or family members who can help you *objectively* weigh the pros and cons about this decision. It's important that these trusted friends and family have a history of being honest with you and will not simply tell you what they think you want to hear. Remember that the people around you may be uncomfortable with your pain too, so they may unwittingly suggest you give the relationship another try whether or not that is in your best interest. It's important that you seek advice from people who have a good degree of emotional stability and can give you an honest perspective without concern for your reaction or their own discomfort for your pain.

Changes

If you are considering reuniting after the breakup, you must think about what needs to change in order for the relationship to succeed. That may require you, your partner, or both of you to make *changes*.

As we discussed earlier, change is difficult, and most people resist it to some extent. Resisting change is perceived as keeping you safe. Even folks who embrace change find it challenging and often push back. You should also be aware of the facts about change. Think about your own history. How much success have you had making changes in your life? Most people struggle with behavior changes (e.g., weight loss, spending habits, how we spend time, eating healthy, exercise, etc.), and the odds of sustained successful change are low.

In addition, people can't change until they are ready. People cannot (or will not) successfully change simply because we want them to. They may want to change to make you happy and may even see the benefit of doing so for themselves. They may try to change, but it won't work until they are ready. For change to be successful, the desire needs to come from inside, not outside.

So, does salvaging the relationship mean your ex has to change or can you now accept them as they are? Needing to see a change from your ex for the relationship to succeed is a treacherous and high-risk situation. If you needed the change then, but don't now, why and for how long will this be true? Consider these questions carefully and weigh the risk or likelihood of change carefully:

- Are they willing?
- Is it a major or minor change?
- Do they have a history of being able to change?
- How much work or effort is needed for the change?
- How long will it take to see the change?
- Can you trust that they will maintain the change?
- Even if they change, can they regain your *trust*? (it's your choice to trust again)!

If there is a need for changes by both parties, you will also need to ask these questions of yourself... and answer honestly. While the deck seems stacked against the odds of success when it comes to changes needed to get back together, there are few things more motivating than love, the possibility of salvaging a marriage or other long-term relationship and keeping a family together to make it work. If you have invested in a long-term relationship, you may want to know you did everything possible to make it work if there is even a fighting chance of success.

More Biases

We've already covered a few of the biases that come into play regarding typical human thought and behavior... but wait, there's more.

On top of the impact of negative emotions, there are several other cognitive biases at play that influence your decision. Moreover, these biases detract from your ability to make a good decision. Unfortunately, these biases that we're about to uncover all stack up in the direction of trying to salvage the relationship. You need to be aware of them, how they operate to influence your decisions, and what you can do to counteract their impact.

Loss Aversion: People go to great lengths to avoid a loss due to the bias known as loss aversion. The desire to avoid a loss may seem like an obvious choice. Afterall, no one wants to lose; we'd rather avoid that outcome. The challenge comes into play when we make choices between an opportunity to win and the potential to lose. This bias to avoid loss is so strong, it can lead you to make choices that prevent you from experiencing something *good*. In other words, as humans, we think of the magnitude of the pain associated with a loss as being so much worse than the joy that comes from a *similar level of gain*.

Loss aversion: the tendency to prefer avoiding losses to acquiring equivalent gains.

Here is how this plays out in terms of a breakup. As you consider the trade-off between going back to your ex after the breakup or finding a new partner, you are essentially weighing the risk of a loss of the past relationship (even though it has already failed at least once) against the promise of a better relationship with someone else in the future (a potential gain). Loss aversion suggests that you will be more likely to try to get back together with your ex to salvage the broken relationship (avoid a loss) than put your energy into the possibility of a new and better relationship (gain). This is true, despite the significant problems that led to the breakup and the low odds of making it work again. As the potential loss is weighed against the gain of a new better relationship, the scale is weighted more heavily in terms of avoiding the loss even when the potential for pain and gain are equal.

Escalation of Commitment: In a relationship, we invest so much time, love, energy, intimacy, and perhaps even finances, we may decide to invest even more additional resources to save it. This may be true, even when we know the relationship is a lost cause. The rational choice in these situations would be to recognize that time spent in the relationship so far is a sunk cost and walk away. You cannot recover any of the resources you've already spent on the relationship. From a rational perspective, the decision to invest time and energy in the relationship at this point should only be evaluated based on the potential payoff of any new resources (e.g., time, attention), with no consideration for the past investment. But we don't do that. And so we are more likely to sink more time into a broken and perhaps irreparable relationship.

Escalation of commitment: a human behavior pattern in which an individual facing some type of loss (with the potential for even bigger losses from a decision, action, or investment) nevertheless continues the behavior instead of quitting and cutting their losses.

Prospect Theory: Another bias that comes into play relates to our strong preference for something we can have today versus what we have to wait for in the future, even when what we get in the future is better. For example, in numerous studies on money, we find that people want their money now, not later (even when waiting would give them *more* money). Obviously, the rational choice would be to wait for more money, but our emotions tell us it's better to have a bird in the hand now than two in the bush later. In this case, the excitement of spending the money on something I want now (and maybe there's a negative past experience of having been burned when the promise of future money didn't pan out) causes us to go for the cash today. Economists would say this choice is not rational, but when you consider the emotions and possible past experience, it seems to make sense. The takeaway is that we are often impatient when comparing something we can have today against something better tomorrow and don't want to delay gratification.

Prospect theory: a behavioral model that shows how people decide between alternatives that involve risk and uncertainty. Most people would rather keep what they already have, than risk the chance to get more later, even when the chance is the same or better.

Let's see how this bias plays out in terms of breakups. Most people are more likely go back to an old relationship in the hope of being happy now (even though they've suffered through the pain of the breakup and there are significant problems with the relationship), than to hold off and invest in a better relationship in the future. Essentially, you are in pain and you want the pain to end. We don't want to postpone our happiness. The relationship of the future is not certain and seems too far away to be something worth waiting for.

In addition, even though your prior relationship wasn't perfect, you may be wondering if what you had with your ex is as good as it gets. If this is your thinking, you may want to postpone your decision until you finish the book. The third part is focused on how to find your ideal partner and get the relationship you want.

As you approach the decision to try again or let go, your goal is to make the best, most rational decision you can. Unfortunately, as you now understand, the odds are stacked against your ability to do that in an unbiased way. Your negative emotions hijack your brain's rational decision processes. Your desire to stop hurting and your human biases nudge you in the direction of trying to get back together with your ex. However, what we know about change makes the path of reuniting very difficult. It is helpful to understand the biases at work, so you can make a more rational decision.

While our biases and resistance to change may seem to paint a bleak picture for the prospects of reuniting, there is hope. This book was designed to help you understand and survive your breakup, learn to manage your emotions, and *find your ideal partner—who could be your ex!*

Actually, if you follow the path prescribed in this book, you could end up in a fabulous new relationship or you may choose to go back to the old relationship but with a much higher likelihood of success. As is usually the case, the only thing you can control is yourself. If *you* are willing to take this journey and make some of the changes suggested, there is real hope for rekindling your relationship. I have seen remarkable results in relationships when one of the partners changes their thinking and behavior. Afterall, when two people are dancing together and one partner changes their steps, the other *has to* change as well. It is the same in relationships. Whether your partner makes changes or not, if you do, the relationship will change.

One final suggestion is to change the way you think about the time spent in the relationship. Instead of thinking of it as wasted time, can you be grateful for the good times and great things that came from the relationship? Then can you think about starting from square one, with a clean slate? Knowing what you know about your partner, are you interested in investing yourself, your time and energy in that relationship, or are you ready to explore the potential of an unknown, different one?

Getting It Right

- One of the toughest decisions to make when a relationship ends can be whether to try to make it work or to move on.
- There are a lot of good reasons to try to salvage the relationship. You loved your ex, have an identity as a couple, a history together, and might even have a family. If go this route, you can at least say you did everything possible to save the relationship.
- There are a lot of biases that come into play with this decision.
- Some of the forces that support a reunion include the desire to maintain the status quo, fear of the unknown, immediate relief of the emotional pain, loss aversion, escalation of commitment, and prospect theory. Being aware of these can help you avoid falling prey to biases and make the best choice.
- Be aware of these biases as you make your decision to stay or move on. While there are a lot of factors pulling you toward getting back together, keep in mind the need for you and your ex or both of you to change. Consider the likelihood of making those changes.

- If you follow the path in the book, you will be better prepared to find a great new partner or successfully reunite with your ex.

Chapter Five:

Understanding the Power of Emotions

Believe it or not, our emotions are the most important thing to focus on to help us get through a breakup in a healthy way.

The typical response to negative feelings is to avoid or under-manage them. The pain of a breakup can be excruciating. For most people, moving past that pain as quickly as possible is a high priority because we want ***out of the pain!*** We try to avoid the negative emotions by ignoring them, numbing the pain, shoving the emotions down, shifting our attention to a new love or a project. As humans, we fiercely resist experiencing emotional pain as if our lives are at stake. This is what under-managing your emotions is all about.

Some of these actions can be helpful in the short term as long as we are ***also*** tackling ***processing*** these negative feelings. However, many times, we do things that distract us from the pain to avoid dealing with the emotions. This will only work temporarily before the negative feelings pop up again and maybe this time more intensely.

Why do we go to such lengths to avoid feeling bad? One reason may be that we don't realize how quickly the emotional pain will end if we allow ourselves to feel them.

"Emotions, by definition, are only seconds or minutes long. And no emotion is built to last, not even the ones that feel so good... they come over us like a wave, and then they dissipate." Fredrickson, (2015).

 Affective Forecasting: is predicting how we are going to feel in the future about situations when making decisions.

Another explanation for why we avoid experiencing negative emotions is related to affective forecasting. Researchers found that people are generally inaccurate when predicting their feelings about situations or things they expect in the future. We overestimate both negative and positive emotions in relation to "bad" and "good" situations or things (respectively) we anticipate. In other words, we think we are going to be more upset by negative situations for a longer time than we actually are. And similarly, we expect to be much happier when positive things happen for a longer than we are.

One research study asked college students in romantic relationships how happy they were and to anticipate how they'd feel if they broke up. The students predicted they would have a big decrease in their happiness if their relationship ended. However, at the end of the study when the students were asked again how happy they were, the students who actually broke up during the study had the same happiness levels as those who were still in their romantic relationships. The study demonstrates that we tend to overestimate how bad we are going to feel about bad events, and that we generally adapt and return to stable happiness levels fairly quickly (Gilbert, et al., 1998).

Putting these findings together, we can see that although negative emotions typically dissipate in a matter of minutes, we think the negative feelings will plague us a lot longer than they do and will feel a lot worse than they do. Again, these very typical misperceptions work against us in a significant way, because we avoid dealing with our negative emotions instead of managing them.

Besides under-managing negative emotions, the flip side is to over-focus. Focusing and processing are two different things. Focusing on emotions (without processing) could include hyper-focus, ruminating on negative emotions, whining, feeling sorry for ourselves, or staying stuck in our emotions for an unnecessarily long time.

Researchers have found that although people who ruminate believe they are solving problems or gaining insight about themselves, it is actually associated with inflexible thinking (Davis & Nolen-Hoeksema, 2000), poor problem solving (Lyubomirsky et al., 1999), and losing support from their support system (Nolen-Hoeksema & Davis, 1999). Of course, it's hard to break out of the pain and grief of the loss of the relationship in the early stages, but it's important to move forward and move past the cycle of negative thinking as quickly as possible.

So how do we get unstuck and reduce the adverse impacts of negative emotions? Instead of over-focusing on or under-managing negative emotions, we need to *process* them (see Chapter 11). As an overly simplistic explanation, this is accomplished by allowing the negative feelings to come into our experience (vs. pushing them away), allowing them to exist, being still and feeling them, allowing/accepting the feelings, letting them wash over us, and then deciding to let them go. Ironically, this process can be accomplished fairly effectively in a matter of minutes. It is really that simple. If you are surprised by this, do an experiment with yourself. In a tough situation, see if you can allow yourself to feel your emotions and any associated physical reactions, instead of pushing them away. There's more help in the next section of the book on Unpacking Emotions, but you can begin to learn more about this in your own experience.

When the emotions are particularly deep, sensitive or painful, this cycle of processing the pain will likely need to be repeated multiple times (maybe even at different times) until the emotions are no longer "charged" or active. You'll recognize when this happens because thinking about the situation will not trigger a negative reaction or cause distress.

If this sounds completely foreign or crazy to you, that is very understandable. Most people have not been taught to effectively manage their negative emotions. We've touched on processing emotions briefly here, but there's more to cover regarding surviving the breakup. The next part is dedicated to providing information and exercises to help you learn to process the emotional mess that comes with a breakup.

Consequence of Not Managing Emotions

If you choose not to deal with your emotions or process them in a thorough way, I am afraid you will regret it. If you ignore them, they may seem like they are gone, but they actually get stored in your body and act as terrorists until they are acknowledged. The negative emotions do not want to be ignored. Chapter 10 on embracing emotions goes into more detail on the ways these stored emotions wreak havoc on your life if suppressed.

For now, it's enough to know that periodically they will be triggered (often by something minor) and will rear their ugly heads again, often by unexpected things (e.g., a song, a fear, a place, a person, etc.), and each time it occurs, the negative emotional reaction is reinforced through your brain's neural pathways.

Now you'll need bigger and stronger actions to push the tough feelings away (e.g., more alcohol or stronger drugs, unfulfilling serial dating and/or sex, bigger and more expensive shopping sprees, or whatever your drug of choice is to numb the pain). These actions are used to protect you from feeling the pain again, but now you may have bigger problems to deal with because, on top of the pain of the breakup, you also have the messes that come from these unproductive cover-up behaviors.

When emotions are not effectively managed, the problems of the past relationship are likely to be ***repeated*** again in the next relationship—the boomerang relationship. This is true regardless of how much work you have done ***thinking*** through what was working and not working. You may have even made some commitments about how you want to think and behave differently. The thing is, you can't think your way out of the pain or into a better relationship. In the world of relationships, emotions rule the day. There simply isn't another path.

If you want a better relationship, you are going to have to learn to manage those painful, uncomfortable, nagging emotions by effectively processing them. I wish I had better news for you. I can at least give hope that if you process your emotions, you have a great chance to have a better relationship in the future and not repeat the mistakes of the past.

Like most of you, I am often reluctant to process my negative emotions, but it's really not so difficult or painful. Getting past my reluctance to get started is really the hardest part and, with practice, it often only takes a matter of minutes. Afterward, I often wonder why I made such a big deal out of it. The anxiety of anticipating it is a lot worse than the experience, and there's freedom and joy when I get rid of the pain and negative energy.

Getting It Right

- Emotions are the key to having a fulfilling, rewarding romantic relationship. Understanding how to manage them and what happens when we don't is a primary determinant of whether or not we have successful relationships.

- As humans, we tend to under-manage emotions (avoid, ignore, numb ourselves, shift attention) or over-focus (ruminate, whine, feel sorry for ourselves, hang on too long). Neither approach allows you to effectively process your emotions.

- Many people think of "processing" the breakup as using logic to think through the dynamics of the relationship, personalities, needs, communication styles, etc. This is an important step, but not sufficient. It is also critical to process the emotions of the breakup.

- Processing emotions is different. Thinking doesn't resolve or release the trapped pain. That only comes from emotional healing. There simply isn't another path.

- Processing means allowing the negative feelings to be present without pushing them away, accepting them, and then deciding to let them go.

- When negative emotions are ignored or avoided, they don't go away, but instead are stored in the cells of our bodies and will reappear when triggered again. This results in a reinforcement that now requires bigger and stronger actions to push the hurt away.

- Very simply and truly: If you want a better relationship, you must learn to process those painful, nagging emotions.

- Fortunately, it is not difficult or time consuming to process your emotions. It is a powerful way to live a more fulfilled and happy life.

Chapter Six:

Tips for Thriving

Now that I've covered some of the psychological impacts of how your thinking may be altering your choices and driving emotions, let's take a look at some of the ways you can survive the breakup and begin to thrive. This is the time to be brutally loving with yourself. It means connecting with people, exercising, eating healthy, spoiling yourself (in healthy ways), and not doing things that feel like obligations. A broken heart requires time and a lot of TLC to heal.

While you may be experiencing a lot of sadness, it may be helpful to give yourself permission and timeframes for mourning. This is important if you are busy and not setting aside time to grieve, or if you are spending too much time being sad, set limits to give yourself a break from the sorrow.

Since each breakup is different, you'll need to gauge when it is best to take these steps. Depending on the intensity of your loss, some of this may be difficult to think about early on, but keep reading, it will help to plant a seed for when you are ready to take action.

Triage: When your breakup occurs and in the immediate days following it, your pain may be so intense that you are not able to function effectively. Remember the analogy of the broken heart being like a broken leg? The emotional injury is real and needs treatment. When you break your leg, you go to the hospital, get X-rays, a cast, take pain killers, put your leg up, and likely need to get some rest and sleep. It would be very difficult to work that day and maybe for several days afterward.

The days immediately following the breakup can be equally traumatic. Acknowledging that the end of a relationship is a real blow, you may need to triage the damage. Remembering the stages of grief, you may also be in shock, especially if the breakup was a surprise. You may not be able to function normally for a while until you are able to think clearly.

For example, it might be best to take a "mental health" or sick day from work to deal with your grief, stabilize your living conditions and family situation if they also changed due to the breakup. This is especially true if you have a job where you can't afford to be inattentive or make mistakes, and you have this flexibility. This is *not* to say that everyone will need to do this or that it's okay to check out of life or your responsibilities. For example, you wouldn't want to take the chance of putting your job at risk right now. Having some continuity in your life is critical.

For many people, work and other obligations (e.g., taking care of your children) can be very helpful to the healing process. They can keep you somewhat distracted from your pain, give you a sense of normality and purpose, and remind you that you are still winning in other areas of your life.

The remaining suggestions are not meant to minimize the intensity of the pain of your loss. Instead, they are provided to help you begin to relieve some of the pain, make the best of the situation you are in, and jump start the healing process *when you are ready*. You are the best judge of when it is time to take action.

Being on Your Own:

After your breakup, you will obviously have more time to yourself. There are some positive aspects to this and some that may be more challenging. On the positive side, there's a great silver lining—more "you" time. Embrace it! To some extent being alone can be a bit of a relief! You have more time to nurture yourself. You no longer have to consider the other person's thoughts or desires in planning your day. You don't have to make compromises about what you want to do or how or when you want to do it. You don't have to take care of them, tiptoe around their moods, or put up with their annoying habits. With the end of the relationship, there are things to think about, decisions to make, feelings to process, TLC needed, and, you now have the time you need to spend on yourself.

On the other hand, you are likely to experience some loneliness. There are also two challenges here worth exploring. First, the tendency to isolate (beyond what is healthy), and second the inability to be comfortable with being alone.

Many people isolate, especially in the beginning after the breakup. You may want to avoid being with others because you feel sad, miserable, or embarrassed about the relationship ending. You might also want to dodge being pressured to talk about it, feel like you are not good company, or avoid burdening others with your problems. The challenge emerges when your isolation becomes excessive. It's really important to balance your alone time with time with other people. The next chapter focuses on helping you stay connected with others.

The second issue is for people who have trouble being alone. Some people think they can't be alone and must have a partner to be happy. They may fill their time with other people, rush to start the next relationship, and do everything in their power to avoid being alone. This overwhelming sense of "need" to be with someone could result in making an inferior choice of partners or an overdependence on your significant other (this may have even been a contributing factor in your breakup). While a partner can enhance your happiness, having one is not necessary. During this time when you are alone, it will be helpful to embrace the experience and maybe challenge your thinking that you need to be with someone else. This is covered in more detail in Chapter 15.

Since you are alone, finding ways to be happy by yourself helps you make the best of your situation. It can also help you get to know yourself better and appreciate your own company again. Doesn't it make sense that if you want to find a partner, it will be easier if you are more emotionally stable and well-adjusted as a single person? This may be an important part of your work in the healing process; find happiness again with yourself being alone. You've been happy before, and you can get there again. Here are some considerations that might help:

Pre-relationship or between relationships: Remember times in the past when you were single and very happy. Maybe that was as a teenager, young adult, or a college student. You may have to think back, but you will likely be able to remember being happy at some point in your life when you were alone. Give some thought to the kinds of things you did for fun, who you spent time with, and what kinds of things made you happy.

In the relationship: Were you and your partner together all of the time? Maybe in the beginning, but over time, you likely spent some of your time doing different things. Your partner may have been a huge part of your life, but eventually other things also became a focus of your time and attention. You had friends, hobbies, activities you did together, and some you did apart. If one of you had to travel and you were apart for a few days or a week, it was not a big deal. You knew how to make yourself happy. You weren't miserable because that person was away. So, there is evidence that you can be happy being alone.

This is not to say that we can't be happy in a relationship, but you won't need a relationship to be happy. It is important that you fully own your happiness—with or without a partner. This is covered more completely in the last part of the book.

Self-Love

Do you love yourself? This may seem like a funny question or a foreign concept, but it's an idea that's worth understanding better. What does it mean to love yourself? Are you appreciating who you are and all you have to offer, or do you sometimes ruminate on the things you don't like about yourself? Do you treat yourself the same way you treat someone you love?

Self-love After the Breakup

You may be great at loving and taking care of yourself, and you can use this breakup as an opportunity to fall more deeply in love with yourself.

Many people however are not great at self-love. You may have actually struggled with self-love long before the relationship ended. Some typical reasons you might find to not value yourself could include lack of financial stability/security, health problems, poor body image, job/career dissatisfaction, an insufficient network of friends, emotional instability, addictions, etc. If there are things you don't like about yourself, you may be living day-to-day with an underlying dislike for yourself related to certain aspects of your life. This form of self-rejection can be very harmful. In truth, this issue may have contributed to the breakup.

Whether or not you previously struggled with a lack of self-love, following a breakup you now have a new situation to challenge it. In the previous section on self-esteem needs, we covered how natural it is to question yourself after the relationship ends. After all, the end of a relationship is ultimately a failure (regardless of who is to blame).

You want to look for the cause to avoid it from happening again, so you try hard to understand what happened. The breakup provides a great opportunity for self-examination, but it is often accompanied with harsh self-criticism. In the process of reflection, it's easy to pick on yourself, be overly self-critical, and blame your perceived deficiencies for being alone. For example, did you make a mistake that caused or contributed to the breakup? Did you ruin your chance of getting married in a certain timeframe? Have you gained weight or plummeted into debt due to overspending? Did you question your ability to attract a mate or maintain a relationship? When relationships end, you may find yourself being critical, frustrated and angry at yourself.

Contrast that scenario with a compassionate and understanding response to the breakup. One in which you are able to balance the wonderful things about you with any of your problems. Through a more empathetic lens, you can see your flaws but not be overly critical. Blake Shelton has a song called "I Found Someone." It tells the story of a woman talking to her ex after the breakup. While it seems like she's referring to finding another partner, in the end, the song unveils the person she found was herself. She says it took losing her love to get there (see Resources for a link to the song). In this sense, the breakup may actually be a gift. You can leverage this opportunity to fall in love or fall more deeply in love with yourself.

Unpacking Self-Love

There are three aspects of self-love: 1) appreciating your value, 2) caring for yourself, and 3) self-acceptance.

1. Appreciation

Appreciating your value means you recognize your worth, without any proof or evidence of accomplishment or success. It is unconditional. Loving yourself means valuing and appreciating yourself exactly as you are, for who you are. You don't need to do anything to earn it. It does not depend on accomplishing your goals or being in a relationship with the partner you want. You recognize your goodness, your humanness, and worthiness, just as you are, without doing anything or needing to change anything. It doesn't stop or lessen when you make a mistake or notice an imperfection.

Fall in love with yourself. What do you like or appreciate about yourself? What are the things your partner loved about you? What do friends, family, coworkers like about you? For most people, it is very difficult to make this list. They can only come up with a short list of characteristics they like, although it's easier to make a long list of things they don't like. Challenge yourself to do this. If the list is short now, come back later and add to it.

> *"I am a human being, not a human doing."*
> *~ Kurt Vonnegut.*

Maybe you have an opportunity to get to know yourself in a different way, see yourself for the first time with fresh eyes. You are special, unique and have a lot to offer.

Can you give yourself the same appreciation, adoration, and acceptance you offer your lovers, your babies, or pets? Perhaps thinking about self-love in terms of the relationships we have or want with other people can offer a valuable perspective. For example, there are parallels between falling in love with a romantic partner and falling in love with yourself. When you meet that "special someone," you typically have strong feelings of attraction, admiration, and appreciation. You want to spend a lot of time with them, have long conversations, learn everything you can about them (e.g., what they like, don't like, their history, what's important to them, etc.). Time flies when you're together and drags when you are apart.

Now consider the way we fall in love with our newborn babies (or a new puppy if that's more relevant). They are completely dependent on us to take care of all of their needs and offer nothing in return—yet they are adored. We love them simply because of who they are, not for anything they do for us. In fact, they are actually quite a bit of trouble, between late-night feedings, crying, and diaper changes, but we love and accept them completely. Our hearts are filled with wonder and awe as we watch them fall down, learn and grow. We don't belittle, criticize, or ignore their needs. These examples of how we love others provide a roadmap of how we can best love and appreciate ourselves.

Compare the way you feel about and loved your partner, children, and pets with how much you love yourself. Are you full of appreciation, giving yourself all the admiration and respect you deserve? Are you able to love yourself, unconditionally, exactly as you are?

2. Self-acceptance.

Most people have a ruthless inner critic, a voice in their heads that makes harsh judgments about mistakes, personality, and physical flaws. Self-acceptance includes quieting the inner critic and treating yourself with understanding and compassion. Becoming more accepting is important for both the recovery from your breakup, but even more importantly for the health of your future relationships.

"Highly self-critical people tend to be dissatisfied in their romantic relationships because they assume their partners are judging them as harshly as they judge themselves. The misperception of even fairly neutral statements as disparaging often leads to oversensitive reactions and unnecessary conflicts. This means self-critics undermine the closeness and supportiveness in relationships they so desperately seek.... Self-critics are also often attracted to judgmental romantic partners who confirm their feelings of worthlessness." (Neff, 2011).

You might believe that being hard on yourself makes you stronger, work harder, or leads you to do the right things. You may feel criticism is justified; we all have flaws after all. Isn't it okay to be aware of your shortcomings and try to be better? Of course, understanding you are not perfect and have opportunities to improve can be healthy; however, there isn't any benefit to criticizing or belittling yourself... and it is actually counter-productive.

In addition, the critical destructive thoughts lead to negative emotions (e.g., shame, doubt, fear, guilt). These emotions influence your actions. The negative emotions are more likely to lead to procrastination, avoidance, and self-sabotage that will keep you from success. Therefore, beating yourself up becomes an additional new barrier to any changes you want to make. Ironically, it creates resistance.

Alternatively, self-acceptance creates positive emotion (peace, comfort, ease, appreciation). These feelings enable change. Positive emotions make you feel motivated, energized, and creative. Self-acceptance motivates through love. Self-criticism demotivates due to fear of failure and the desire to avoid any further painful criticism. By letting go of the proverbial "stick" used to beat yourself, and instead showing compassion and appreciation, you open the door to enable the changes you want to make (e.g., lose weight, apply for new jobs, eat healthy, date healthy partners, etc.).

Changes are hard enough to make without heaping on more obstacles! Criticizing yourself is not a winning strategy and will actually prevent you from moving forward in a healthy way to get the relationship what you want. The next section identifies ways to increase your self-acceptance.

> *"The curious paradox is that when I accept myself just as I am, then I can change."*
> **Carl Rogers, On Becoming a Person**

Awareness. A good place to start is with an awareness of the ways you may be overly critical of yourself. You may not even be aware of the self-defeating messages that are swimming in your head. After all, you've had that voice in your head for many, many years. The words and messages may be flying "under the radar" without you even being consciously aware of them, but they are influencing you regardless.

You may need to start this process by stopping to listen to the voice inside. This is called meta-cognition— thinking about thinking. For example, you might have a thought running through your mind like, "I wasted three years in this relationship; how could I have done this again; no one good wants me, I am not attractive?" Notice how none of these is accepting of yourself or kind. We need to tune into the voice and become aware of what it is saying in order to change it.

Decide on Fierce Self-love. Make a decision to end any judgment or criticism for whatever you've said, done, or don't like about yourself. Fierce self-acceptance takes courage to love yourself without limits, no exceptions. Can you accept the parts of you that you don't like? Can you forgive your mistakes, overlook physical flaws, and be patient and kind when you are hurting? Rather than listening to your critical inner voice, try talking back to your inner critic.

When you love someone else, you focus on what you like about them. Sometimes you do this so well their flaws become invisible. Can you learn to love yourself in the same way? Or can you accept yourself the way you do your children or pets—overlooking or forgiving mistakes and physical and emotional flaws? Replace your critical thoughts with hopeful, nurturing, and positive thoughts

Self-Compassion. Practice being more compassionate to yourself. Research shows that self-compassion is related to steadier and more constant feelings of self-worth and happier and more satisfying romantic relationships (Neff, 2011). It was also associated with less social comparison, the need to retaliate for perceived social slights, or the need to be right. You could write a compassionate letter to yourself or keep a self-compassion journal to focus on shifting from harsh, critical self-talk to kinder and gentler thoughts.

Treat Yourself Like a Friend. Talk to yourself as gently as you would talk to a cherished friend. If you heard a friend talking harshly or critically to themselves, you would probably think or say, "I hate to hear you talk to yourself that way" or "You don't deserve to be treated so meanly." When you beat yourself up, what you are doing is similar to bullying and is not empathetic to your own situation. Establish a rule that you will not say anything to yourself that you wouldn't say to a friend or loved one. In other words, take the stick you are using to beat yourself and throw it away; begin being kinder to yourself. Talk to yourself like you would a cherished friend! If this harsh criticism is happening for you, it's time to stop.

Choose to Be Patient with Yourself. This means not rushing through the healing process. It is painful and uncomfortable, but the process shouldn't be rushed. Following the suggestions provided here can accelerate the process and make sure you will be in a better position the next time. However, it won't take away the need to take some time to heal. If you broke your leg, you wouldn't expect it to heal overnight. We all know and accept that bones take time to heal, but somehow, maybe because we can't see or touch our emotions, we expect our hearts to have miraculous recoveries. You can practice patience by making a decision to be kind and forgiving to yourself. Offer yourself kind words and thoughts, give yourself extra time, and plenty of rest. Lower your expectations of when you should heal or start dating again. In fact, try to eliminate any of the "shoulds" you place upon yourself and your recovery process.

I felt a lot of internal pressure to quickly move on, get over the relationship, be happy again, and find my next great love. I was very tired of hurting. I was disappointed in *myself for not being more emotionally healthy or healing faster. I was also super-frustrated and hurt that my ex moved on so quickly and was dating **a lot**. I hadn't stopped thinking about him; I couldn't just turn it off... even after 6+ months. The competitive side of me hated that he seemed to be doing well much faster than me.*

A big part of my healing came from accepting myself and being patient with my journey. Comparing myself to him was not helpful. After I was more patient and accepting of my pain, my ability to process my feelings, and the speed at which I moved forward, things got easier. I wrote this book while I was on this journey, which wouldn't have happened if I would have pushed through the process. In the end, while it took some time, I learned to be more patient and accepting of myself.

3. Self-care

Self-care is the way you demonstrate your love of yourself. It can mean prioritizing time for yourself, saying no to obligations that don't feel good, not allowing others to speak or act disrespectfully to you, or taking care of your needs before the needs of other people.

In the case of small children or others who are dependent upon you, many times their needs must often come first. However, it doesn't mean denying your needs and always prioritizing their needs over your own. Instead, you can recognize that you have needs and meet them as soon as possible. Valuing and taking care of yourself provides a good role model for your children and may help to break a generational/societal norm in your family. Many people have spent years caring for others and have not learned or taken the time to care for themselves. Before we go any further, there is a big difference between self-care and selfishness.

Selfishness. The word selfish has a negative connotation, suggesting that a person who puts their own needs first is bad or uncaring. This perspective is often taught by religion, family systems, and by society. Many assign a high value for sacrificing yourself for others. Societal pressures make this especially true for women. But if we are all valued and worthy humans, isn't taking care of ourselves necessary too? This is not to say that caring for others is not important. In fact, being of service and giving back to others can be fulfilling, rewarding, and enhance your health and happiness levels (see Chapter 7).

However, if taking care of others is out of balance with taking care of yourself (e.g., *always* putting others' needs first, not making self-care a priority), it's really hard to authentically love others well because you are depleted. People who consistently put others' needs ahead of their own may be exhibiting co-dependency (to learn more, see Resources).

Self-love is necessary if you want to be fully present and available for other people. When you love and care for yourself, you are better at loving others. You understand more about what love means, your own needs are met, and you have the energy, capacity and ability to give to others.

Inside or Outside? Self-love comes from inside (e.g., understanding and accepting yourself). Remember self-care is a way to demonstrate your love by taking care of yourself (e.g., treating yourself to a massage, buying yourself that bracelet or watch you've been wanting). Keep in mind that these external forms of self-care are expressions of love, but self-love can only come from within. Getting these things can be wonderful, but it's important not to confuse getting external things with self-love, which only comes from inside.

Body Image. When a relationship ends, you may be focused on any perceived physical flaws (e.g., the size of our nose, or breasts for women, teeth that aren't straight, being overweight, wrinkles, etc.). Many people turn to diets or plastic surgery to become more attractive and lovable. Research, however, has shown that weight loss or plastic surgery does *not* improve happiness.

One study compared women who chose to have cosmetic surgery with women who did not and found that existing mental health issues (depression, anxiety, deliberate self-harm, attempted suicide, and illicit drug use) predicted the likelihood of having the surgery. In other words, the women with more mental health issues were more likely to have cosmetic surgery. In addition, the women who had surgery had even higher ratings of anxiety, depression, eating problems and alcohol use than they did before the surgery (Von Soest et al., 2011).

Another study followed a group of overweight adults over a four-year period. Part of the group gained weight, some maintained their weight, and a third group lost weight. Researchers comparing these groups found that the group that lost weight had significantly more depressive symptoms and lower well-being scores than either of the other groups (Jackson, et al., 2014).

These studies point to the idea that although someone may take these actions to become more attractive, they do not result in their feeling more lovable. This is not to say that we shouldn't have the surgery or lose weight, but if you do it without learning to love yourself differently, you are not likely to be happy. Taking this route probably just postpones the inevitable but necessary work of learning to love yourself more.

Improving Self-Care. An important step here is to make a list of the ways you like to be loved. For example, it could include getting flowers delivered, enjoying relaxation time together, sharing a sunset or walk on the beach, etc. The list is as individual as each person. You are an expert in what you want and how you want to be loved, so spend some time thinking about it.

Some of you may have lost touch with what makes you feel loved. It's important to rediscover what you like, what excites you, and what gives you energy. If you don't know what you like and this is a new concept or if you've lost touch with yourself, it's a good time to explore. The next few paragraphs give you a place to start. Incidentally, this is an excellent exercise to help you get ready for your next great relationship.

What makes you feel loved, what do you need and like to do? What did your ex do that made you feel loved? While this may seem painful initially, it will be worth the effort to think about it. As a side note, when you consider what makes you feel loved, you may notice that in reality, your ex may not have loved you in all the ways you wanted to be loved. After all, no one is perfect. Use this information to find ways to give yourself what you want and need. You can also set an intention about what you want in your next relationship (see Chapter 12).

As you make your list, think of any other ways you would like to be loved. The five languages of love could be helpful in identifying some of those categories. These include words of affirmation, quality time, receiving gifts, acts of service, and physical touch. There is an online test to help you determine which type you are (see Resources).

Love languages: describe how we receive love from others, including words of affirmation, acts of service, receiving gifts, quality time, physical touch.

Dr. Gary Chapman

The point is that you know what you like and what makes you feel loved and appreciated. You can probably see where this is going. What if you were to do the things you loved for yourself? Our goal here is to substitute the love you got from your ex with a new way of loving yourself. What if you treated yourself the same way you would like to be treated by a new love interest? Another benefit is that when we treat ourselves well, we demonstrate our value to others in our life and model how we would like to be treated.

Can you go on dates with yourself, dress up as you would for a date, do the things that you would enjoy with a date, but do them alone? For example, you could go to a comedy club to laugh, sit under a tree in the park, take long walks, go to art exhibits, take bike rides, etc. When you do this, notice that you *don't* need to be with someone to enjoy the experience. You can enjoy your own company.

I rarely took time to prepare a nice meal for myself. It seemed like a waste to spend so much time on me. Part of my effort to fall in love with myself was to make incredible meals for myself. This was similar to what I would do for a special man I was interested in. I also took a lot of walks, sat on a blanket under a tree in the park, went to a movie theater by myself (which was for some reason particularly intimidating, but also very good), and wandered through some local museums. I have been so surprised at how much I could enjoy these activities.

Does it matter who the love is coming from? After all, isn't the feeling of being loved just as wonderful when it comes from your child or a best friend or maybe from a parent? If your child brings you a handful of wildflowers they picked, isn't that similar to the feeling of getting flowers delivered from a romantic partner (especially after you've gotten past the infatuation phase)? Of course, the relationship is different, but if we concentrate on the feeling of love, there are definite parallels.

I'd argue that you can be indifferent to where the feeling of love comes from. If you have a belief that you need to feel love from a partner, challenge that feeling. Perhaps there is an opportunity to begin to experience more love by recognizing and allowing it to come from a multitude of people and experiences (e.g., yourself, family, friends, people in your church, neighbors, etc.). What is really important is feeling love, not the source of the feeling.

*I loved holding hands with my ex. I remember fondly the first time he reached out to hold my hand; it was after we parked the car on our way to breakfast on a cold morning. I **loved** that feeling and never got tired of it. So, I just visited* *my grandson and one day he reached out and held my hand and guess what? I felt the same rush.*

There is a "watch-out" regarding self-love related to the choices you make about how to care for yourself. Avoid self-care options that sabotage your overall health. Some examples include going on a shopping spree (when you can't afford it), drinking excessively (due to the hangover or behavior you may regret afterward), overeating compulsively (with negative feelings about weight gain), having sex indiscriminately (if it leads to regret, guilt, comparisons with your ex or other bad feelings—for you or for those you partner with). The key is to avoid situations that create negative feelings afterward. You may choose these to avoid the pain of the breakup, but these types of actions can pile on by creating additional new problems.

Winning

You may not be feeling like you are winning in the relationship game right now, but truthfully it's just a temporary setback. While the relationship was a big part of your life, it is not your whole life. Keep a winning mindset about the other parts of your life that are working and have confidence in your future happiness. When you are ready and able to follow the roadmap in this book, a great partner and relationship will appear for you.

In the meantime, turn your attention to the many other ways you are winning in your life. Give yourself a boost by finding something else you can do in another area of your life to feel like a winner (e.g., complete an online class, learn to play a song on a piano or guitar, make a cake from scratch, train to run a 5k or half marathon). Create reasons to celebrate and feel good about yourself. What would make you feel proud, successful, and like you are a winner?

For me, one example was running or walking every day. No matter what else was going on or how badly I felt, at least I could say I lived up to my commitment to exercise. Of course, there were so many side benefits that came from the daily exercise, getting outside, breathing, and I NEVER regretted the decision to run after I started. There was some pride felt in maintaining that commitment. I also made spending time with myself, processing my pain a priority. There were a lot of insights that came from this work. Although it was difficult, I always felt like a winner when I took the time and had the courage to tackle another belief, thought pattern, or emotion. I felt like a winner when I learned something or let go of some pain.

Forgiving

In addition to finding something that makes you feel like a winner, forgiveness is another key component to getting back on track with your life. It is important to forgive **both** your ex and yourself. You may have done or said something that hurt your ex, or you may have not been able to give your ex something they needed (e.g., a commitment). You may not have thought you needed to forgive yourself before, but it can be very helpful.

You may not like the idea of forgiving your ex; after all, they hurt you, and they may not deserve to be forgiven. Read on, there are some good reasons to consider doing it anyway.

Forgive for the right reasons. Forgiveness is a way to release negative emotions (e.g., anger, hurt, fear or resentment) that are blocked due to the trauma of your breakup. You may not see or feel this blocked energy, but it's there and it's sabotaging you. The decision to forgive releases blocked negative energy and helps you let your ex go, so you can move on faster. You forgive them for you because you don't need to be mired down with pain, anger, and resentment. Forgiving your ex can bring the closure you need to the relationship ending.

Perhaps your ex hurt you or did things to hurt the relationship, but you still care for that person, and you don't want them to feel sad, remorseful, and guilty. That is a good reason to forgive, but it is no longer your job to care for them.

Maybe there is something inside of you that wants to use this forgiveness discussion to rekindle the relationship? If this is the case, be brutally honest with yourself about your intention and what you want the outcome to be. Forgiving your ex does not require a letter, text, phone call, or in-person conversation with them. You don't need to say those words to them. In many cases it will be more harmful than helpful to communicate your forgiveness to your ex, and it could backfire in a number of ways.

For example, your ex may not feel they did anything wrong or need to be forgiven. This could put them on the defensive and your good intention to forgive just ends in another argument. They may be ultra-sensitive to what you say and how you say it, so your words and their meaning could easily be twisted, creating more angst for both of you. This would likely be a very sensitive conversation, and if they react inappropriately, it could set you back from the ground you've gained in your healing. One alternative that allows you a sense of healing but avoids any potential problems communicating with your ex is to write a forgiveness letter that you don't send.

True forgiveness may take time. You may know intellectually that you want to forgive but may not be ready until you are... well... ready. You may also need to forgive multiple times. You might forgive, but then find yourself feeling angry or resentful again. This is okay. Again, you need to accept yourself.

Don't forget, it is equally important to forgive yourself. Offer yourself the same compassion you would offer someone else you love. There is a technique you might find helpful in your work with forgiveness. It is known as the kindness meditation, and there are several versions that originated from an old Buddhist practice (see Resources section). My shorthand version is to offer this wish with your greatest spirit of love and compassion. Start with offering the wish to yourself and then offer to your ex, with no expectation of anything in return.

- May I/you be happy
- May I/you be loved
- May I/you be peaceful
- May I/you have an easy life

You can also offer this silently to anyone else in your life (e.g., children, parents, friends, strangers you pass on the street). It can be especially powerful for anyone you are in conflict with or don't like. You can offer this meditation daily. It has a way of helping you move from anger and hurt to a place of compassion and forgiveness.

Getting It Right

- There are many things you can do to move from survival mode to thriving. These practices can help relieve some of the pain, make the best of the situation, and jump start the healing process *when you are ready*.

- The most important thing to do is to engage in self-love by:
  - o Appreciating who you are, fiercely accepting yourself with any flaws or mistakes, and practicing self-care.
  - o Being critical of your imperfections and mistakes does much more harm than good, and gets in the way making any changes you want to make. To speed your recovery, be kind, compassionate and patient with yourself.
  - o Fall in love with yourself—remember what is great about you. Do the things you love to do, go where you love to go, make yourself happy (e.g., consider buying yourself flowers).

- Several of the other key tips include:
  - o Embrace being alone and find happiness with yourself as a single person. If you have trouble doing this, recall times both before and during the relationship when you found happiness alone.
  - o To counteract feelings of loss, find new ways to win again.

- o Forgive both yourself and your ex. Forgiving your ex benefits you... do it for yourself.
- The best part is that you don't have to be miserable or spend months or even years grieving the relationship. These practices can help you thrive now.

Tips for Thriving

Chapter Seven:

Helpful People

Remember Maslow's Hierarchy of Needs from Chapter 1? The primary need activated by the breakup is for love and belonging, so connecting with people is your lifeline right now. Try to make some form of meaningful connection every day. These people can help fill that awful void left by your partner's absence.

Connecting with other people helps to get out of your pain and self-pity. It helps meet your need for belonging and love in other ways and with other people. It puts your life in perspective to see everyone has complexity and challenges in their lives. You can see that you are not alone in experiencing the challenges of the human condition.

Another benefit of connecting with others is getting some diversity of thought. As was covered previously, our emotions hijack our rational thinking ability. Being stimulated by different people and different ways of thinking can help combat some of the irrational thinking biases that occur after a breakup and sometimes help us make better decisions. One caveat would be to be sure those perspectives come from safe and trustworthy people. These are people who have proven that they can tell you the truth even when you don't want to hear it. Of course, it's helpful if you are ready to listen to what these trusted others have to say.

At the end of day, when your love life isn't very gratifying, there is something to be proud of if you can say you connected with one or two people in a meaningful way.

These other people can meet some of your love and belonging needs.

Connection Opportunities

There are plenty of opportunities to connect with other people:

- Happy hour after work
- Walk with a neighbor
- Phone call to a parent on the drive to work
- Breakfast, lunch, dinner with a friend
- Lunch with a work colleague
- Yoga class with an acquaintance
- Invite someone to coffee after church services
- Hallway conversation with someone in your building or on your block
- Volunteer activities with others

These are just scratching the surface of possibilities. Think about what you need from these connections (see examples of needs for connection below). You will likely need a balance of all of these. Having a mix of these needs met in different relationships can accelerate your healing. Don't worry right now if you don't have a large enough network; we'll tackle that next. Don't get down on yourself if that is the case. Friends often fall by the wayside in long-term relationships. This is something you can guard against going forward. Promise yourself you'll maintain your friendships better in your next relationship, but for now, you have an opportunity to renew some past relationships too.

Consider how these connections with friends and family can meet some of your needs:

Hanging out: You and your ex spent time together and lots of it. That's one of the things that happens when people fall in love—they want to be together. So, when the relationship ends, there is a *lot* of time to fill. Not all of the time has to be spent with other people but being alone all of the time isn't healthy either. You will need to spend time with people, just hanging out, helping to fill the big hole in your calendar.

Who are the people with whom you can shop, cook or share a meal, watch a movie, take a walk, visit a museum, garden, go to the farmer's market? You'll need people who you can hang out with, talk with casually and maybe not even discuss the breakup (except superficially). This is helpful because you need a break from talking about the relationship. In addition, your friends will get tired of hearing about it.

Filling weekend/prime date time: If you aren't ready to date, or don't have a date, but want to get out, you need people to go out with. Who are the people with whom you can attend events like a wine tasting, craft fair, or a concert?

The best option here is for friends who have your back and will watch out for you as you start going out again and meeting people. These friends understand your vulnerability and may help you steer clear of people and situations you have told them you want to avoid. Or maybe these friends can encourage you when you are ready to take a risk again.

It's important to note that you may want to avoid people who try to parent you, judge you, or tell you what they think is best for you. Rather, you want to be around people who genuinely respect your wishes as you've described your intentions *before* going out.

In terms of identifying these trusted friends, keep in mind that friends who are the same sex or opposite sex can be great companions. You may believe that they need to be single friends, but married friends may enjoy getting out too and could be better than single friends who could become distracted by their own relationship needs and interests.

I had a mistaken belief that going to a concert, movie, wedding, or art fair wasn't the same if I was going with a friend or family member instead of a romantic partner. However, that was an illusion. I realized this while I was in a relationship by examining my feelings at concerts with and without a partner. I thought about how much I was enjoying myself both ways.

I noticed that the amount of fun I had was not necessarily related to the person who was standing next to me, as long as it was a person I liked and enjoyed being with. If I felt free to sing along and dance, I had a pretty good time. I also found myself freer to make friends with the people sitting around me when I wasn't with a partner. This was a surprising win. I met people who came from different cities for the concert and they were as big of fans as I was. It was nice to be with people who shared the same love of this music as I did. This wouldn't have happened if I would have been with my ex.

Somewhere along the way, I learned that there was a stigma attached to going somewhere alone or with friends instead of a significant other. Don't get me wrong, I still remember fondly how nice it was to walk into the concert with his arm around my waist or look into my eyes when they played a favorite song, but the truth is that the music is still the same. What I had to fight was the idea that being with a friend was not as good. There is really no rational foundation for this thought; it was clearly a mistaken belief.

Increasing your fun quota: You need to balance your time grieving with time having fun. What do you like to do and do you have friends, acquaintances, or family members you like to do it with? I had a couple of young nieces who were very entertaining (and available). I could count on having fun and laughing when I was with them. A side benefit was that their mom and dad appreciated the time off. If you don't have this, consider joining a meet-up group. Finding people who enjoy the same activities as the ones you like could be very rewarding.

If you aren't sure what you like to do, think back to what you enjoyed as a child. Is there something you'd like to do again? Examples of these activities could be to join an intramural sports team, take a painting class, or build something. Find out what your friends do for fun and consider joining them.

Often in life we don't have enough time to do the things we enjoy. Following a breakup, we have a lot of free time. Leverage this time to increase your fun instead of naval gazing about the lost love.

Move and exercise: Most humans find moving to be physically and emotionally therapeutic. Invite a friend, neighbor, or coworker to take a walk, go to an exercise class, bike ride, go bowling, or play golf. The possibilities are endless. Seeing and appreciating something beautiful in nature is nourishing and healing, so moving outside is particularly helpful.

Conversations with trusted friends: We all need someone who can help process grief and negative feelings. Probably the most important people to have in your life are the trusted, emotionally mature friends who can listen and not judge, give advice when you are ready and open to hearing it, give a balanced perspective, or maybe say nothing when you just need someone to be there for you.

This is a really tall order for a friend, and you may not have people in your life who can fill this need. If you don't have friends who are insightful, you don't trust, or who will not tell you the truth, you could make some new friends or see a competent professional to give you a wise perspective (see Chapter 11 for information on professionals). Whatever it takes, having a trusted confidant is important.

Giving back: Another category of activities is volunteering or giving back in some way. It can be helpful to forget about yourself for a while and give back to others in need. Giving back can recharge your batteries, fill your love tank, build your self-esteem, and increase the meaning in your life. Helping those less fortunate can be the best medicine if you are feeling sorry for yourself.

When individuals volunteer, they not only help their community but also experience better health (e.g., greater longevity, higher functional ability, or lower rates of depression). Corporation for National & Community Service (Grimm, et al., 2007).

You might look for people who are already engaged in charitable activities you would find rewarding to join or think about people you know who need your help. Do you have family members, neighbors, or people in the community who need your talents or time?

If you don't personally know of anyone who could use your help, you could try your church, or an environmental, community or civic organization. You could read to students at school, hold babies in a hospital nursery, care for animals in a shelter, or visit people in a retirement home who could use some company. Depending on your interests, you might help out with a political campaign or join a team to build a Habitat for Humanity® house. The possibilities here are endless. If you are really ambitious, why not join a board or organize a new group or initiative yourself?

You might also be feeling like you are running on empty and have nothing to give, but it doesn't have to take a lot of energy, time, or even a completely positive attitude. Sometimes an extra pair of hands is enough help. Find the opportunity that matches the time, interests, and talent you have.

When a relationship ends, finding purpose in service to others or a significant cause can be an important way to meet your needs for belonging, self-esteem, and self-actualization. Even though your intent may be to help others, there is an amazing payoff for your own healing.

Cast a Wide Net

Following the end of the relationship, as much as you don't like to admit it, you will likely be lonely and, yes, needy. The prior section just outlined a lot of opportunities and ideas for connecting with other friends, family, neighbors, colleagues, and acquaintances. Of course, it's okay to rely on a few close friends to help you through the toughest parts of the breakup, but you can overburden them if you rely on them as your primary "go-to" folks to fill *all* of your needs.

Overdependence on one person or even a few is not a healthy approach for several reasons. First, remember that you may be particularly needy, and even your closest friends and family can tire of hearing about your problems. If they can't be there for you the way you want them to, it may actually reinforce the disappointment and/or feeling of rejection you have about your romantic partner. With your primary relationship over, these folks are some of the most important people in your life now. Reinforcing disappointment or rejection with these important people in your life could leave you in a very bad place and set you up to create some strong negative beliefs about trusting others. In addition, overburdening a friend or small group of friends is simply not fair and is not taking care of your relationship with them.

Try to rely on these few closest and healthiest people in your life to help you with the ***most important*** needs (e.g., confidant, processing your emotions), and allow other people to be there for you with less intimate and critical needs (e.g., play, exercise). Since you will have so many needs, you need a wide network of friends and associates, so let's take a look at who and how you can connect.

Start by making a list of your friends, family, neighbors, acquaintances, colleagues, etc. This might include people you haven't seen or talked to in a while. Who have you been meaning to connect with but haven't had the time? Who would you like to catch up with? You should also consider professional colleagues and acquaintances from work. It's also a great time to make new friends and acquaintances.

Now try to match them to your needs that we've just covered. Don't forget you can also make a plan to do some of these things by yourself. Add your name to the table where you would like to challenge yourself to do things alone.

Need:	Who?:
Hanging out	
Weekends/prime dates	
Fun/adventure	
Exercise/movement	
Confidant	
Giving back/volunteer	

Other Considerations

Positive vs. negative: Following a breakup, you are in a negative place. You've experienced a loss and there is a lot of sadness and grieving. As much as possible, try to tip the scale of negativity in the other direction by surrounding yourself with healthy, happy people. If you have negative people in your circle and on your list of contacts (e.g., complainers, pessimists, gossips, people who judge and chastise you), spend as little time with them as possible.

Set the right expectations: Don't set yourself up for disappointment. Expect that many of the folks you reach out to will say no or won't be available. Don't turn that into another rejection; expect it as normal. It's not personal; people are just busy—remember you used to be the same way. If you reach out and they don't respond or don't make it a priority, assume the reason is most likely something in their life; it's not about you. So, let it go easily. At least you made an effort, followed through with a commitment you made, and they can follow-up later if they want.

Professional colleagues: It's a great time to reach out to work and other professional colleagues to schedule a happy hour, coffee, or lunch. As a huge added benefit, the networking opportunities will most likely boost your career, with the added personal benefits of helping you connect with more people and get through some of the most challenging times.

Expand your network: It might be time to make new friends. You might check out some of these ideas:

- Meet-up groups in your area. This is a great way to meet someone who has a similar interest (which is an automatic way to find people who have something in common), and possibly renew or explore some new activities or hobbies in which you are interested.
- Classes: Take a class (e.g., cooking, tennis, guitar, salsa dancing, etc.) or a workshop on something that interests you.
- Staycation: What parts of your city have you always wanted to visit? Take an architectural tour, visit parks, scenic overlooks, local breweries or wineries, museums, farmers' markets, local events and festivals.
- Sports: Can you join a sports team? This is a great way to get your social and exercise needs

met. The team is a ready-made social connection. If you don't know people on the team, invite someone out before or after a practice or game. Get to the practice early or stay late to begin to get to know some of the players. For example, my sister goes to a pick-up pickleball game on Friday nights, where they rotate through whichever players show up.

- Fun: Plan a party or invite some friends to join you at a local bar holding a trivia night or go dancing at a honky-tonk. Invite different groups of friends/family/colleagues—encourage them to bring other friends. Keep it informal, no RSVPs necessary. Just keep it open.
- Volunteer events and activities: Become a docent at a museum, work at a booth at an art fair, become a greeter at church, etc.

I understand that all of these ideas take effort, and when we aren't feeling good about ourselves, this can be hard, but *do it anyway*!

Connection obstacles: Isolation is a big obstacle. Connecting with others takes effort, and after a breakup, people have the natural tendency to withdraw and isolate. There may be multiple reasons: sadness, embarrassment, not having people to do things with, uncomfortable doing things alone, needing to take time to figure out what happened, etc. In addition, the emotional turmoil that comes from the breakup drains us of physical energy. Some days dragging yourself out of bed, taking a shower, and getting dressed to get out and meet with someone seems overwhelming. I get it, but caving into that and opting for isolation is not moving you forward.

You may also feel like you are not good company, but schedule time with people and *go anyway*. Since you are on an emotional roller coaster, you can't really predict exactly when you are going to be on a high or a low, so you don't need to worry about this or tell people in advance of your meeting. In addition, you don't want to create an unhealthy pattern of repeating a negative statement about yourself. If you find that you are struggling when it's time to meet, and if it gives you relief, during your time together let the person know that you are struggling and might not be the best company. Most people will have empathy and will not mind. Every single time, I felt better after getting out and connecting.

Lost Friends: You may have lost touch with some friends over the course of the relationship, and it may seem awkward to contact those folks after a significant amount of time has passed.

You might be embarrassed because you're afraid they'll think you are only calling because you broke up and are now lonely. The main concern here is to be sure you are genuinely interested in seeing them again, and if it goes well, and both parties are interested, renew the relationship. You don't have to decide before you contact them if you want to make a commitment or not. Things change and people change. It's okay to test the waters.

Don't take it personally if you reach out and they don't respond or are too busy to meet. As was already mentioned, you should expect this to some extent, especially from folks you have not stayed in touch with. These folks might also be the most likely to say, "Yes, let's get together" and then cancel at the last minute or don't see it through to find a mutual time at all. Again, it's okay; this is not a time to judge others. You are looking for a renewal of friendship, and it's okay if the other person isn't in the same space.

Surprisingly this did not happen with the friends I contacted, which tells me I may have been unnecessarily concerned and harsh on myself. I also learned that most of my friends missed the relationship too, and in truth, it goes both ways. Their lives got busy as well and they also could have picked up the phone, sent a text, or reached out via social media. Most of the friends were just glad I called, and it was amazingly simple to pick up again right where we left off. So again, while there may be some reluctance to contact lost friends, do it anyway.

How to Connect

Besides simply telling you to just do it, here are a couple thoughts about how to approach these connections. First, you have to prepare and have the right attitude. Become curious and excited as you think about connecting with people—it is part of healing. There is something to learn from everyone. Listen to different perspectives, appreciate the sense of connectedness from just being with another person, and look for things you like about everyone you meet. Taking the time and making the effort to do this will help with your healing. If you are lonely and driven only to meet your next partner, you might not see the benefit of connecting with so many other people. These people may not help you reach your goal in an obvious way, but this puts you on the path to a better relationship in the future.

What you need is to help your heart heal, and the way to that is by connecting with safe people and beginning to open your heart to them. At every meeting, ask yourself "How can I be of service to this person? How can I let them know what I like and appreciate about them? How can I learn from this person and then let them know how grateful I am they make the time for me?" Taking on this mindset will change you over time. Your altruistic thinking will, in fact, come back to you and accelerate your readiness for romantic love again (and the right partner).

Think of it this way: Are you ready to meet your next mate? Although you are broken-hearted, are you your normal fun, interesting, and open self? Or are you in some state of emotional bankruptcy, filled with sadness, possibly mistrusting others, experiencing self-doubt, fear, etc.? If you were to meet the perfect person today, would they fall in love with you or run? If you think you can hide your current broken state, I'm suggesting you might be wrong, and even if that might be true, would you be starting a relationship built on trust and honesty? Through the process of connecting with others first, you will regain your positive energy, confirm your own value, and become more ready to appreciate others.

Next, it's up to you to set time with others. It's your job to take the initiative to reach out and schedule the meeting or call. Make it easy for people to connect with you. Invite them to connect but make the invitation light; don't appear desperate. Likewise, make it easy to say no or back out if they need to. If the people you make plans with back out, you should let them off the hook graciously, but don't back out yourself—no matter how bad you are feeling.

1. When making contact, keep it light. You can say, "I was thinking about you lately and wondered if you

might want to get together?" or "It's been a while since we've talked; I'd love to see you if you are interested in getting together."

2. Offer several options over the next couple of weeks to get the negotiation started on finding a day or time (this is often the most challenging part). End with a "no guilt" clause. For example, "No worries if this doesn't work for you, or if this is a bad time, I just wanted you to know I was thinking about you."

3. Let people off the hook easily if something comes up for them. When in doubt, frame the meeting as tentative. "Let's set a tentative time to meet and check in to confirm that day."

There were two times that were the most challenging for me: 1) weekdays after work, and 2) weekend (date) nights. I missed connecting with someone about my day, having dinner together, or just facing my empty home again. Sometimes I enjoyed going to a coffee shop to work or hang out just to be around people. Occasionally I might strike up a conversation with a stranger. I met some interesting people or at least had some easy human connections to keep me from feeling lonely. Scheduling happy hours or dinners with colleagues was a great way to take the edge off of the "after work" times. I often set up happy hours with colleagues after work because that seemed to be the easiest, most convenient ways for them to meet and it filled my lonely evenings. However, I always let their preference guide the timing. I happened to have a lot of time on my hands.

For weekend nights, I often looked ahead for events coming up and then during the week I sent a group text to friends inviting them to attend with me. I always ended with

"no obligation, just thought you might be interested."
Typically, at least one person responded back that they
wanted to go, but even if no one responded, I stuck with my
plan and went alone.

Be committed. Make plans and take these actions to connect a lot. Even if it's not something you want to keep doing forever, it's important for the short term to get you through the temporary loneliness of the breakup. I made sure I was making a meaningful connection with at least one person once a day for six months (and that was through the COVID-19 outbreak). When you make plans and commit to a meeting date/time, you are more likely to follow through when the day comes even if you don't feel like it. For people you haven't seen in a while and with whom you are trying to re-establish a relationship, it's particularly important that you don't flake out and cancel. If there is a real emergency situation, be clear about the reason and immediately put a plan in place to reschedule ASAP. Remember, don't back out yourself—no matter how bad you are feeling.

Even after I got over feeling sad and lonely much of
the time and was doing a pretty good job of taking care of
my needs for relationships and belonging on a regular basis,
I still found myself needing a connection boost periodically
for at least a year after the relationship ended. There were
times when I slacked off and noticed myself isolating or
expecting too much from one person (i.e., someone I was
dating). One of the things I did to combat this was to set up
some monthly reminders as a way to ensure I was scheduling
time with people in my circles.

While this might seem contrived for many people,
because I'm a planner, it was helpful for me. I segregated

"my people" into three concentric circles. I didn't need a reminder to connect with the people in my inner most circle—I usually went out with them at least monthly. However, for the people in the next layer of my network, I set up a reminder as a trigger to reach out and put time on the calendar with them every other month. For people in the outer circle, I set up a reminder to try to connect quarterly. Because I can gravitate toward isolation, it was helpful to set up a system to stay in front of this rather than getting behind. I think my friends and colleagues also appreciate my proactive contacts.

Talking About the Breakup

When you get together with others, remember to focus the conversation on them. Start the visit by telling them you want to know what is happening in their life. Listen well and ask questions that show your genuine interest. If they ask, tell them about *other* things that are happening in your life too (e.g., your family, your work, your activities and interests). Remember: there is more to your life than the breakup!

You may not be prepared to share intimate details about your pain with people you haven't seen in six months, a year or longer, and they most likely don't want to know that much about the situation either. If it seems appropriate, you can let people know about the breakup but it's probably best not to belabor or dwell on it. Remember the importance of surrounding yourself with positive thoughts, people, and interactions to counteract the powerful influence of the negativity bias. Whenever possible, use your time with others to escape your grief and put your attention on something fun, exciting, happy and interesting.

People will likely ask about your relationship. Prepare in advance and think about several responses that feel safe, so you will be ready if you decide to share or when someone asks you a question. While you may be incredibly emotional for a long time, there may be several things you could say without tearing up.

For example, you might say, "My two-year relationship recently ended and, yes, it's been tough over the holidays, but I'm focused on taking care of myself and learning what I can from the experience." If they press for details, you might say, "If you don't mind, I'm glad to have a break from thinking about it, so I'd rather not talk about it now." This allows you to be genuine and honest but not disclose more than you are ready to talk about. If you are really concerned about the reaction from friends or acquaintances you haven't seen in a long time, you don't have to mention it at all. It's probably safest to wait until you see how the conversation is going and how trusting you feel with that person during the conversation before deciding if you want to mention it or not.

If you are operating under the belief that you need to talk about the breakup a lot to vent and heal, *this is a mistaken belief*. While it is important to process the grief, talking about it over and over to everyone is not the answer. In fact, this will only create a new memory trace, a habit of thought, and will only serve to reinforce and reactivate the pain repeatedly. The next section of the book focuses on processing the emotions to deactivate the pain for good.

Getting It Right

- Connecting with other people can be one of the most satisfying and fulfilling parts of our lives. Fortunately, it is also one of the best ways to recover from a broken relationship.

- We have a psychological need for love and belonging (which is lacking when a relationship ends), so connecting with people is a great lifeline to meet that need.

- Isolation after a breakup is common, so you'll need to make an extra effort to connect with people. Make a commitment and a plan to make it happen.

- If needed, you can broaden your network of connections, reconnect with old friends, or make new friends. Volunteering can be a great way to fill your need to connect with people, put your problems in perspective, and give more meaning to your life.

Helpful People

Chapter Eight:

Helpful Thoughts

After the breakup, it is highly appropriate to spend time evaluating your relationship and why it ended. You want to understand what worked so you can repeat it in your next relationship and what didn't work so you can change it. While this chapter is focused on thinking or analyzing the relationship it's important to note that processing or analyzing the relationship is different from processing your emotions (which is covered in Chapter 11). Be aware that too much focus on your head (thoughts) without dealing with your heart and your emotions can result in harmful trapped negative emotions. Here are a few other "watch outs" to help you with the relationship processing:

- It's important to have a compassionate learning mindset when you do this work. A person with a learning mindset places a high value on learning and is focused on continuous improvement. They look at new challenges as opportunities to learn. Instead of getting frustrated when they fail at something, they view mistakes as part of the learning process and keep going.
- If you are consumed with negative emotion, it would be better to wait until you are less "under the influence" of your strong emotions (remember emotions can limit your ability to think clearly).

- It is easy to be defensive and blame your ex, (we all have a human desire to protect our ego). However, both people play a role in the relationship and in the breakup. If you aren't able to honestly look at your responsibility in the relationship ending, you will miss a great opportunity to learn. If this is the case, *there's a good chance you'll repeat the pattern.*

- Alternatively, it's not helpful to be overly critical about your mistakes or any character defects. Chapter 6 offers tips for self-love and acceptance to help you with this issue.

- Look fearlessly at the dynamics of the relationship. The truth behind the end of the relationship may not be as obvious as it appears to be. For example, are you thinking that the relationship ended because of a stormy fight instead of a pattern of emotional immaturity, or are you naively idealizing the relationship and ignoring the problems?

- You might find yourself focused on going over the details of who said or did what. This is only useful to a point; over-analysis is not helpful. In addition, the specific words used in a fight may not be as important as the underlying issues. It might be better to step away to see the big picture and get a fresh perspective.

How much time do you spend thinking about your ex and the relationship? If your ex was in your life for a long time, it may be difficult to stop thinking about them regularly. You spent a lot of time together, they were a big part of your life, and so it's natural to think about them a lot. However, at some point you will be better off minimizing thoughts about your ex and moving on.

Let's draw a distinction between thoughts you initiate and those you don't. When you are evaluating the relationship, you are making a conscious decision to think about your ex. You are in control of your thoughts and how much time you spend thinking about them. The thoughts you initiate as part of an honest analysis of the relationship make good sense. Since you are in control of those thoughts, you can start and stop them as appropriate for healthy relationship processing.

Sometimes thoughts are triggered by a song, a place you visit, something you read, or by a memory. In these cases, there is an association with something in the environment that triggers the thought. These thoughts are automatic and are difficult to control because an external stimulus is driving the activation. If you want to move on and minimize being triggered by these thoughts and the corresponding emotions, you could avoid the places you went together or stop listening to music that reminds you of them. This may not be possible in all cases, but it could be helpful in the short term. The associations with places, people, and things will weaken over time on their own since your ex isn't there to continue to reinforce them.

The third category of thoughts is probably the most problematic and important to consider. Sometimes thoughts about your ex or the relationship can occur seemingly without any trigger at all (or at least without any triggers you are aware of). These thoughts seem to come randomly out of the blue. The thoughts could be about anything: something they said or did that you miss, a memory about a good time together, replaying an argument, or plans you made together about the future that won't happen now.

For example, if you are out enjoying a beautiful morning walk and a thought about your ex pops into your head, how does it make you feel? Does it disrupt your good mood? Do these thoughts seem to come too frequently and feel obsessive? The result of a continuing barrage of thoughts may create an extended sense of sadness and grief, over and over again. In addition, the repetition of thought might lead you to draw a false conclusion that you are still in love or can't live without them. However, that's not necessarily what the stream of regular thoughts means. It may just mean that your brain has established a pattern or habit of thinking that is automatic. There is a repeating memory trace in your brain.

The good news is that neuroscientists tell us we can actually change this wiring in our brains. These patterns can be reversed or overwritten by being more intentional and replacing the negative thoughts with more positive thought patterns. A deeper discussion of the neuroscience behind this process is beyond the scope of this book, but if you want to learn more, check out the Resources at the end of the book. In addition, if this is a big issue for you, the last part of the book does a much deeper dive into how to change your thoughts for the future that might be helpful now.

I was flooded with thoughts about my ex for a very long time. In many ways, I felt like a victim to my own thoughts. Every time I thought about him, I felt some level of longing, disbelief, sadness, or anger. Although this is very normal, over time, I knew these thoughts were keeping me from moving on. I wanted them to stop but couldn't seem to control them.

There were a few important things I learned. First, while I couldn't control the thoughts that seemed to randomly pop into my head, I could control the thoughts I initiated! For a while, I shared my story with some people. I am typically a very private person. However, there were two reasons I reached out to acquaintances. First, I was in an urgent need to find a place to live, so I reached out to several people who I thought might know of temporary housing. Second, in my disbelief, grieving the loss and sense of unfairness, I was looking for other people to help me make sense of this and maybe tell me I wasn't crazy.

But I knew early on that repeating the story was not helpful. It simply stirred up the pain and longing over and over. For example, when people asked how I was doing I might jokingly say, "Well, aside from being homeless I'm doing fine."

After a couple of months, my ex and I had a brief text exchange, and he correctly pointed out that it must be serving me to be the victim. He was right and I appreciated his insight. So my new mantra became: **"Tell a different story.**" I stopped saying jokingly that I was homeless, talking about the breakup, or only talked about it briefly. If I ran into people who knew me and it was appropriate to update them, I'd just say, "My boyfriend and I broke up."

The second important thing was reframing how I thought about the relationship. Instead of grieving the loss of a great relationship, I began being grateful for the time I had with him, all the things I learned, and the happiness I *felt. I also tried to be grateful for the brutal way he broke up with me. Looking back, it was what I needed to move on with a clean break and little risk of reuniting.*

This may seem like a simple thing, but the act of reframing the way I was thinking and talking really changed a lot for me. What I noticed was that feeling the loss, frustration, and the pain kept me stuck and seemed to perpetuate the negative thoughts. Feeling appreciation helped me accept the situation and move forward. It wasn't easy and it took time to make the shift, but I could feel myself letting go more. Accepting the end of the relationship and appreciating the good was definitely more helpful in terms of my healing.

Finally, when a thought about my ex popped into my head, I tried to halt it as soon as I noticed it and replaced it with a different positive thought (this is an example of rewiring). My replacement thought was, "I'm free"— celebrating the independence of being on my own. It was simple and easy to remember. It was important to have this positive thought ready to go, so I could stop the thought about my ex before it hijacked my mood with a negative emotion. If I would have needed to consider a good replacement thought option each time a thought about my ex came up, it would have taken too long and a sad or frustrating emotion might have taken hold.

Our opportunity here is to examine our thoughts and retrain our minds to be more selective about the thoughts we replay. Recognize that it is within your control to choose how long this goes on (even if the thoughts seem to be habits and keep popping into your head randomly). Have you noticed your thoughts related to the breakup lately? What are they about (topics/content)? What is the frequency, the intensity? When do they come up? What triggers them? How do you feel when you think of your ex or the breakup? Are there thoughts you would like to change?

Do an experiment and track your thoughts throughout the day for several days. If that seems too difficult, try it for 30 minutes, an hour, or several hours. This exercise goes a long way to uncovering your thought patterns, and without knowing what they are, you cannot begin to take steps to change them.

In the aftermath of the breakup, we can also make matters worse by establishing new habits of negative thoughts. For example, if I am continually thinking about how hurt I am, or what a terrible human being my ex was, I am laying down a new memory trace and reinforcing it over and over again. Repeated negative thoughts about your ex and the relationship may not be serving you. If you want to move on but have established this new pattern of thinking, it makes it more difficult to start feeling good again.

The bad news is that the negative thinking will not just plague you immediately after the breakup but may continue indefinitely because of the new habits of negative thoughts. The frequent bombardment of these thoughts that cause pain are like a form of relationship PTSD. You can change these patterns of negative thinking! Again, the last part of the book goes into more detail about how to change your habits of thoughts if you want to skip ahead and tackle this more now.

Getting It Right

- It's important to spend time thinking about the relationship, what worked, what didn't—as objectively and compassionately as possible. It's important to have a learning mindset vs. a blaming mindset when you do this work.

- There's an opportunity to take an honest look at the relationship dynamics including each person's role in the breakup. In most cases both parties have some level of responsibility. It takes a lot of courage to own up to your responsibility for the breakup, but it also jump starts the healing process too.

- Thoughts influence emotions. If you want to reduce some of your sadness and anxiety, work to focus your thoughts more productively and avoid relationship PTSD. For example, focusing your thinking on hope for the future, self-love, and winning will lead to a better life than ruminating on your pain, mistakes made, or anger at your ex.

- Like behaviors, thoughts can be habitual too. Be intentional about breaking negative thought habits and creating the right positive repeatable thought habits. Tell a different story.

- Understanding and then leveraging the power of your thoughts can enable you to get the wonderful life you deserve.

Chapter Nine:

Making Changes:

Beware of Short-Term Gain with Long-Term Pain

The end of a relationship can be a great motivator to help us make some changes in our lives. Some examples include making personal changes (e.g., cutting or changing the color of your hair, starting or changing an exercise program, plastic surgery), taking on new projects (e.g., home improvements, building something, going back to school), making major changes in your life (e.g., changing careers/jobs, or moving to a different city). There are a lot of things we do when we are in pain in order to feel better.

There are definitely some positive aspects to making changes in your life, particularly when you have been intending to make these changes for quite some time. If you haven't had the time to make the changes you want or moved forward with your plans for some other reason you can now leverage your situation to take action. The pain of the breakup (and the free time you now have) can give you the motivation to push forward. Another benefit is that you need a break from negative emotions. These actions can give you the needed relief from pain and offer something positive on which to focus. Making a change can help you feel like a "winner" again, especially if you successfully complete or accomplish something. This is particularly helpful if you are feeling rejected. Often taking a break from the pain, allows us to reach a new level of insight or clarity about a situation.

However, there are a couple of big "watch outs" regarding these changes. In some cases, these activities or changes may distract you from your pain but can do more harm than good. For example, if making a dramatic change distracts you and numbs your pain to the extent that you don't feel the need to process your emotions, it has done you a disservice. Be certain that you make processing emotions your first priority. Build in time to allow yourself to feel and process your grief throughout the course of any project or change you undertake, or as soon as possible afterward.

Also, depending on the scope and size of these changes, they may create more chaos than relief or clarity. If the changes add too much stress to your already fragile state (remember a broken heart is as serious as a physical injury), it may be very difficult to make this change as successfully as if you were under normal conditions. Of course, there are also situations in which you don't have a choice about making a change (e.g., if you are co-habitating and you need to find a new home). However, in these types of situations, is there a way to minimize the chaos of the decision? For example, can you move somewhere temporarily until you have time to give more thought to where you want to live when your head is clearer? Would it be possible to stay with a friend or family member for a while (an added benefit is being around other people)?

Here are some general rules of thumb to consider for major changes: First, ask how you feel when you think about the change. Is your mindset positive, excited, and happy? Or is it coming from a place of fear, desperation to stop hurting, and uncertainty about how you are going to manage the change? When you make a decision from a fear-based perspective, you will typically feel constrictive about your choices. Decisions made with a clear mind feel more expansive, with more excitement about the opportunities. This could be a helpful way to test whether you are on the right track with your decisions.

Another consideration is when you want to start. Are you ready to be successful with a major change? What is the downside to laying the groundwork by thoroughly investigating and planning for the change, or even taking some initial steps forward, but waiting a week, month, or longer to start? Postponing the chaos of embarking on something so big that it gets in the way of your healing may be a better option. Another idea is to talk with a trusted friend about their perspective on starting this change now. Someone who isn't as close to your pain may be able to give you a clearer perspective.

I was scheduled to retire from my full-time job of 14 years and start a new consulting practice when my ex and I broke up. I was extremely excited about starting a new career. However, the relationship ended one month before Christmas and six weeks before my retirement date. Since we had been co-habitating for six months while my condo was under renovation, I had to find a temporary place to live. Between ending the relationship, not having a place to live, and managing the renovation, it was a pretty stressful time. I made the decision to postpone my retirement. I hated to tell people at work about my problem, but I needed to have one area of my life that was stable (even if it was the job I was leaving). Fortunately, they were understanding and flexible. It was helpful to give myself permission to wait until I was in a more stable position to make the move.

Escape Behaviors

There are other types of behaviors people engage in that are clearer to see as harmful (both short and long term). For example, excessive drinking, binge watching television, shopping sprees, emotional eating, or serial dating may help to escape pain in the short term, but they also have the potential for harm. Emotional eating is a very common behavior associated with breakups. The section that follows gives a deeper dive on emotional eating, but the dynamics and issues are similar with the other escape behaviors.

Granted, these behaviors can be a great escape if they are done in moderation as a shorter-term break from your grief or overthinking your problem. However, as we touched on earlier, many of these distracting behaviors feel good in the moment but can lead to more bad feelings afterward that just pile on to your already negative feelings and mindset. For example, going out and drinking may help you talk to new people more easily, forget your troubles for a few hours, and have some fun. But excessive drinking can lead to being hungover the next day and bad decisions made while intoxicated (e.g., saying hurtful things or having sex with someone when you would not have made that choice sober). Most of these types of behaviors feel good in the moment, but end with feelings of regret, shame, and may sabotage your self-esteem.

If these behaviors are harmful, why would we engage in them? We do it because we know they work. We have experience with these behaviors relieving our pain temporarily. Sometimes we are willing to sacrifice the long-term problems for a short-term gain (remember prospect theory—people would rather get something today than wait for something better later)?

Finally, there are some behaviors you may be tempted to engage in that have no redeeming value even though there may be a temporary sense of vindication. The cost for these behaviors is simply too high. For example, retaliation is a no-win game. You may want to pay your ex back for what they did but striking out at them will not help.

Let me make a distinction here between your feelings and your actions. Your feelings of anger, resentment, hate or revenge are perfectly valid and justified. These feelings are not wrong and may even be helpful for your recovery. The next section can help you acknowledge and move past those emotions in a healthy way. The caution here is about *acting* on those emotions in a retaliatory way that can do more damage to you.

A moment of relief is not worth the guilt, embarrassment, or potential retaliation that may come back to you. Another harmful behavior is trash talking about your ex. While sharing the truth about your ex with your closest friends and family in as much of an honest and dignified way as possible is important, it is not helpful to talk poorly about your ex with acquaintances or strangers. After all, you liked or loved this person. Acquaintances and strangers probably don't want to hear the dirty laundry about your ex and may judge you for being so negative. They may wonder how you talk about them behind their backs. In both of these cases, take the high road and refuse to stoop to negative behaviors. Finally, remember the idea in Helpful Thoughts on "tell a different story"? Repeating negative thoughts over and over keeps us stuck.

Stalking or harassing are also behaviors to avoid (e.g., repeated unwelcome contacts to your ex, confrontations in restaurants, attacks on social media, etc.). While this may be obvious, I mention it because people in emotional distress do not always see the obvious. Also, it could be easy to move from a relatively harmless behavior into something more destructive pretty quickly. There is no opportunity to win here. Instead focus on letting your ex go.

Emotional Eating

When negative emotions are painful, people want relief and may eat compulsively to feel better. Emotional eating is one of the most common examples of ways we try to quiet our painful emotions when relationships end. We see this frequently depicted in movies or on television shows when someone is crying while eating a quart of ice cream right out of the container after a breakup. Can you relate?

Since it is such a common occurrence but also very harmful, I want to spend some time delving into this further and share ways to overcome it. First, to be clear, what most people want when they are eating emotionally is to stop their pain and fill the "hole" in their gut. They typically crave sweet carbohydrates (e.g., cake, brownies, cookies, chocolate) or salty foods (e.g., chips), not carrots or celery. These carbs have little nutritional value but give us an immediate feeling of fullness (a proxy for filling the hole and the emptiness) and the sweets give us a blood sugar surge for quick energy. The immediate sense of relief and temporary distraction from pain is the win. Unfortunately, while there's a benefit in the short term, there's a longer-term problem.

Since the eating isn't related to hunger, you are most likely overeating. This leads to weight gain, which can result in self-esteem issues. Body image and self-esteem may already be issues you are struggling with after a breakup. Emotional eating compounds the problem. It only feels good temporarily and almost always ends with feelings of shame, guilt, regret, and frustration… more negative feelings to pile on. Finally, and maybe most importantly, it doesn't solve anything. The emotion is still there and will come up again later.

Why do we do it? There are scientific and psychological reasons for the harmful behavior and awareness of them can be helpful. While the precise scientific explanation of this phenomenon is beyond the scope of this book, a brief high-level summary can shed some light on why we engage in emotional eating and what we can do about it.

Emotional eating results in several chemical reactions in your body. Cortisol, dopamine, and serotonin are a trifecta of hormones that get triggered. When we are stressed, cortisol kicks in and floods the body. It can make you crave sugary, fatty, and salty foods. Dopamine, often considered the feel good hormone, is a neurotransmitter (chemicals responsible for transmitting signals between the nerve cells of the brain). It kicks in when you anticipate something good happening, like eating brownies or a chocolate chip cookie. Finally, the hormone serotonin (also a neurotransmitter) helps regulate your mood as well as your sleep, appetite, digestion, learning ability, and memory. Carbohydrates (including chocolate) can boost serotonin levels, which can improve your mood. So there is a scientific rationale for our desire to comfort ourselves with foods (particularly sweet carbohydrates and salty processed foods like chips).

 Emotional eating: the practice of consuming large quantities of food -- usually "comfort" or junk foods -- in response to feelings instead of hunger.

In addition to the scientific explanation, the psychology behind emotional eating points to the impact of eating—it provides relief from our pain and stress. Stress, sadness, grieving, and loneliness lead to anxiety. Remember the fight-flight response? Eating has a way of calming that anxiety. It provides comfort. You may consciously or unconsciously be making a deal with yourself when you eat emotionally. The conversation might go something like this: "I am hurting. I don't know how to make this pain stop. If I eat these sweets, I'll feel better. I know this because it has worked for me before. I realize there may be consequences, but I can't stand this pain right now and it has to stop. Give me that cookie." We might also say to ourselves, "This pain is unfair; I'm tired of it and I want it to end. I deserve to have something good. Eating this sweet will taste and feel good. This is how I'm going to take care of myself right now. I'm willing to make this trade-off to numb this pain now." This is another example of the prospect theory bias: giving up a better long-term gain (maintaining your health) for a less attractive short-term gain (immediate satisfaction).

It takes a certain level of self-awareness to become conscious of the thoughts and feelings that are leading to emotional eating. If you are plagued by this practice, you may notice that it has become a habit or automatic behavior. Your body is taking over in response to pain and stress by applying the solution that it thinks (or has learned) will best relieve your pain. It can be almost as automatic as removing your hand from a burning stove. If you have been emotionally eating for a long time, you probably have established a memory trace that gets triggered when you want to relieve pain.

After emotional eating, we feel calmer, breathe easier, and are able to slow our bodies' reactions down. The combination of the scientific and psychological satisfaction provide relief to our stress and anxiety. Eating also offers a distraction from the emotional pain; it's something to do. It requires us to physically grocery shop or find food at home, prepare it, serve it, and eat or get in our cars and go out to eat.

Emotional eating has been described as a way to stuff our feelings. Can you picture this analogy? The act of putting food in our mouths is a way of pushing your feelings back into your body where they can't escape. Eating keeps those feelings locked inside of us instead of letting them come out to be released. It quiets the pain so it can stop screaming about how much it hurts.

There are several takeaways to consider regarding emotional eating. The first is to stop beating yourself up for doing it. You are not weak or stupid. There is a scientific and psychological reason for the behavior. It's actually a very logical response that has worked in the past and helps to temporarily relieve some of your pain. Beating yourself up about it is adding insult to injury and actually makes it worse. Try being forgiving and accepting of yourself.

Second, it's important to understand that emotional eating is sabotaging behavior. The temporary relief has a **high** cost long term. Become aware when it is happening; observe your thoughts and actions before and during the emotional eating episodes. If it is automatic behavior for you, you'll need to introduce something new to break up this response pattern. Stop the behavior by finding a better way to take care of the emotion. For example, call a friend, take a drink of water, meditate, or take a walk. Try journaling before and/or after to uncover the conscious and unconscious thoughts, assumptions, and beliefs at play, so you know how to tackle them. Emotional eating can be a really big deal for some people, and if this has been a habit for a long time, it will likely not go away overnight. Leverage Part 2 of the book on Unpacking Emotions to process your emotions in a healthier way.

I was a recovered but a life-long emotional eater when my relationship ended. Over the nine months after our breakup, I had gained about five to seven pounds but worse yet, I recognized the return of some emotional eating habits. I had to put some of the same interventions in place as I mentioned above (e.g., fierce self-acceptance, processing emotions, journaling). However, there were a couple of behavioral science practices I added. I learned that I have to introduce something different or novel into my automatic scripts to slow me down enough to break the pattern.

I put a big note on the fridge (where I often ended up when I had feelings) with three questions:
1) What are you feeling?
2) Can you resolve the issue?
3) What else can you do to feel better now?

Secondly, I moved my "go-to" choice for emotional eating (potato chips) to a new cabinet and put them in a sealed container and then in a larger sealed container. After doing that, instead of habitually grabbing the chips and quickly eating them, I had to search for them, and then open each of the two plastic boxes I hid them in. To be honest, it didn't always work, but adding a couple of extra steps was sometimes enough to slow me down and break the reflex of eating emotionally. These behavioral science tricks gave me a moment to breathe, so I could allow myself to think more rationally about my other choices.

Ready to Date Again?

Starting to date again is the last example of an activity that could be really good or could cause more challenges if you aren't ready. This is a very big question, but it doesn't have to be a question that is overwhelming or something to worry about. Frankly, understanding your readiness for dating is going to be a bit of a trial-and-error process. However, don't worry—you can't get it wrong. If you start dating and then find that you aren't ready, you can pause and then go back to dating later. There are also all kinds of options about how to date (e.g., taking it slow or jumping in with both feet, various online dating options, exploring renewals of old relationships or dating people who have been friends, etc.). Keep in mind, Part 3 of this book will help you prepare for your next relationship. However, there are some particular considerations around dating that are relevant for someone who has recently ended a meaningful relationship.

How do you know if you are ready? First, there are some great benefits to getting back on the horse, so to speak, and dating again. Beginning to explore another romantic relationship, or at least getting out and meeting people, can be a good way to move forward and potentially relieve some of the sadness and loneliness. After all, dating can be fun and exciting. Going on dates may start to provide a level of companionship that is missing and distract you from ruminating on the loss of your ex. It can also feel like you are doing something productive in your search for a replacement. Discovering that you are desirable again can give you a big self-esteem boost if you are struggling with that. However, don't forget that self-esteem comes from inside. If you are tempted to rely on others to make you feel great, resist. Instead, grow your self-worth by becoming more aware of your own value, interests, likes, and what makes you happy. Then if others admire and appreciate you, it is icing on the cake, not the cake itself.

Dating can fill the void and get you started on the right track. *Just make sure you are doing it for the right reasons.* Let's consider what could happen if you date before you are ready or for the wrong reasons. Here are some "watch outs":

Do you want to date? Are you excited about dating again? If you aren't ready or interested in dating yet, don't. Wait until you are ready. Don't date because you are lonely or feeling like you should or because others are telling you it's time and pressuring you to go out. However, if you are at the one-year mark (following a divorce) or six to nine months after a shorter-term relationship, for example, and you don't feel like dating again, there may be more at play. If you have not sufficiently processed your emotions, it is likely you are not interested in dating because you are afraid of being disappointed or hurt again. Are you still in love with your ex? Could you be harboring hopes of getting back together? Are you so focused on self-improvement that you are waiting to become perfect before you embark on a relationship again? This is also a form of fear about being hurt again.

I wasn't ready to date after my breakup for four to five months. My ex was dating heavily about a month after the breakup (it may have been sooner; that's just when I heard about it). It bothered me that he was dating so quickly, and I felt a sense of competitiveness about it. Comparisons with others are real killjoys. I remember thinking, "What's wrong with me, why aren't I dating yet?" I wanted to heal and be ready for the next relationship before him, but it didn't happen anywhere near that way.

The truth was that I wasn't interested in dating for a long time. I wasn't turned off by the idea of dating or afraid to have another relationship; I was hopeful about that. I just couldn't imagine going out with a man or being attracted to someone for a while. I guess I just needed time to stop loving him and to fall in love with myself again. I learned for me love wasn't just a faucet you just shut off because you have a fight and breakup. The important thing was waiting until I was interested in dating on my own (not because I was lonely or feeling competition or pressure from anyone else).

While dating can be fun and exciting, if you are dating to avoid your pain or dealing with your emotions, it will likely take some of the fun out of it. Using dating to distract you from dealing with your pain is a temporary solution. It can be like an addict looking for a fix. It is very human to want to avoid pain, but procrastination doesn't mean you won't have pain; you are simply putting off the inevitable.

If your primary reason for dating is about connecting with people and companionship, that can be healthy, but it's dangerous to think about your dates and/or potential partner as your sole source of companionship. This is a great time to expand your network of friends to get more of your needs met by others, as was covered in Chapter 7. If you do this, you will go into the relationship with a healthier sense of balance and the relationship has a better chance of surviving if your partner isn't expected to meet all of your needs.

How will you show up? Are you ready to meet the perfect mate? The emotions associated with the end of the relationship call into question your ability to put your best foot forward. As previously discussed, you are probably not using your best judgment, making rational choices, or even being great company when you are grieving. While you are meeting new people, you may find it hard to have a conversation without thinking or talking about your ex. You don't want to "bring your ex" (figuratively) or your relationship baggage on your dates.

Rejection is part of the game. One of the most interesting things about dating is that rejection is built in. It's a normal, expected part of it. It's not my favorite part, but it truly is inevitable. We meet people, try them on, so to speak, and then move on if they aren't a good fit. If you are ready to date, you **must** be ready to reject and to be rejected and **not take it personally**. If either of these is a problem for you, then you are probably inviting trouble and are not yet really ready to date again. If you are feeling sensitive about being hurt or hurting someone else, you might want to wait until you are a bit more desensitized. If you fail to do so, dating can add to your negative feelings and may lead to a delay in your overall longer-term healing.

Besides, what's the rush with dating? If you aren't ready, you are probably not showing up the way you want to, may be overly susceptible to the biases we've discussed, and then are likely to have a lot of disappointing experiences vs. rewarding ones. In the worst-case scenario, you could be jumping into dating without processing your emotions. If you do this, *you are highly likely to repeat the relationship issues of the past.*

There are two important notes here. First, while rejection is inherent in dating, you can do everything humanly possible to be respectful, kind, and honest with the people you date (and yourself) to avoid making the rejection any more painful than it needs to be. Part 3 on finding your ideal partner will provide some tips for this.

The second note concerns having sex while dating. Sex can be a wonderful, as well as a complicating, factor with dating. There are so, so many different considerations, interpretations, assumptions, innuendos, and implications associated with having sex. For example, I knew a person who had a rule about never having sex until the third date, and someone who said if someone won't have sex with me on the first date, there won't be a second date. You might be concerned about getting a bad reputation, sending a message that you liked someone more than you did, performing well, taking care of your partner's needs, or STDs. It might be best to postpone until you are really clear about what you want and need in relation to sex and are on emotionally stable ground. There is more on Sex and Dating in Chapter 16.

Getting It Right

- Leveraging the motivational power that often comes from a relationship ending can help you make important changes you want to make in your life. There are many benefits to using this opportunity for good!
- This section is full of great tips to keep you on the right path and avoid some very tempting pitfalls.
- Making a big change or taking on a large project on the heels of a breakup can provide a break from negative emotions and give you an opportunity to feel like a winner again; however, it may also create more chaos than you are ready or able to handle. It might distract you from the important work of processing your emotions in a nonproductive way.
- Escape behaviors are big "watch outs," and often lead to more harmful consequences.
- There are both scientific and psychological reasons for emotional eating (a common escape

behavior), so pay attention and increase your self-awareness about this behavior. Process your emotions to prevent unhealthy behavior.

- Dating can be a great remedy to what is ailing you, but it can also create some additional challenges. Make sure you are dating for the right reasons. Ask yourself these questions:
  - o Are you ready? Have you processed your emotions?
  - o Are you still in love with your ex?
  - o How will you show up?
  - o What is your rejection tolerance?

Making Changes

Part 2: Unpacking Emotions

What exactly are emotions and why are they important? They are simply your feelings (e.g., love, anger, fear, joy, frustration, etc.). They are important because they dictate your state of mind—basically, whether you are happy or unhappy and how often. They also influence action. Positive emotions give us energy to take initiative, go to work, meet with friends, and take care of ourselves. Negative feelings drain energy; they may lead you to procrastinate, worry, stay in, and not want to take care of yourself or others.

You can expect to experience the full spectrum of emotions in life from deeply happy to deeply sad and many feelings in between. While we've been focused on the negative emotions related to a breakup, not all of your feelings will be negative. You might also feel some sense of relief because no relationship is perfect and there were probably some problems leading up to the breakup. You might also enjoy having time to yourself, and you may have some hope about your future.

Another important thing to know about emotions is that they snowball, so the happier you are, the more you'll be happy. The more you sit in negative feelings, the more negative feelings you will have (remember the negativity and confirmation biases). While no life is void of negative emotion and there are biases increasing the likelihood of experiencing negative emotions, there are ways to tip the scales in favor of more positive than negative feelings. Part 3 of the book will focus on your positive emotions and how to enhance them.

Since most people do not like having negative emotions, and would do almost anything to avoid them altogether, this section will focus on overcoming the negative feelings. They are notoriously problematic. In fact, it would not be unusual if you are even having negative feelings about reading this section! You may be feeling uncomfortable, skeptical, anxious, impatient, or frustrated with the prospect of dealing with your emotions in a different way. Let me start by saying that this is a universal problem with which every human suffers.

One of the challenges is that no one teaches us how to process emotions as children (or adults for that matter)! This can change in future generations, but for the majority of this book's readers, your parents and teachers were probably not skilled at dealing with their emotions, nor did they model or teach you the best ways to manage yours.

In addition, there is some negative stigma around having emotions, particularly for men. For example, many men are taught at an early age not to cry or show emotions because it is not masculine. So, they learn to suppress them. Women have issues with emotions too but haven't had to deal with the same societal norms as men related to expressing emotion.

Most of us have learned to cope with our emotions to some degree, but it seems to be a skill very few people master completely. For the rest of us, learning to manage our emotions is a lifetime journey. It's important that you take responsibility for learning better ways to manage your emotions, but don't blame yourself. If you have resistant thoughts about having or dealing with emotions, it's in your best interest to overcome those thoughts.

In Part 1 of the book, you learned that emotions are *really* important to understand and manage to maintain healthy relationships. In this part, you'll learn more about how your negative emotions impact your life and how to manage them, so they don't manage you. The goal of Part 2 is to make processing your emotions as simple, pain free, straightforward, and effective as possible. The best news is that it does *not* have to be difficult, and it will make an immense difference in your life. So, read the material provided here, and try some new things going forward.

Doing this work will help minimize the negative feelings and help you prepare for your next fabulous relationship in which you get exactly what you want.

Part 2: Unpacking Emotions

Chapter Ten:

Why Embrace Emotions?

"What? My relationship ended; I can't stop thinking about my ex. I'm sad, lonely, hurt, angry and worried. I can't think straight. It's hard for me to get through the day or be hopeful about the future. Now you want me to embrace these feelings? You have got to be kidding!"

You may be thinking similarly. However, this is the path to success. Embracing and processing your emotions is critical to cope and move forward more productively when relationships end. This chapter helps you better understand your negative emotions and why managing them is so important. It lays the path forward to manage them in a healthy way.

Negative emotions wreak havoc on us in the aftermath of a breakup. Most people have some underlying feelings which may include a combination of loss, anger, sadness, regret, loneliness, fear, betrayal, hate, worry, confusion, or feeling unloved.

On top of these underlying feelings, there may be many things in your environment that remind you of them, thus bringing up more feelings. For example, you hear a song you both liked, or you drive by their favorite restaurant, or see a common friend. The triggers are everywhere, especially when you've been together for a long time. Simple things you did together (e.g., cooking dinner, raking

143

the yard, walking the dogs) can all become painful reminders that you are not together anymore. Special events (e.g., weddings, family reunions, work picnics they attended with you) and holidays may also remind you of them and can be especially challenging. Each of these external stimuli can trigger negative feelings (e.g., sadness, regret, anger, remorse, etc.) and keep the emotions fresh in your mind.

Finally, as we covered in Chapter 8 on Helpful Thoughts, in addition to memories or thoughts that are triggered, unwelcome thoughts about your ex may seemingly pop up out of the blue. This barrage of thoughts may restimulate your pain and can keep you from moving forward.

These thoughts and the related emotions are painful, so we want to minimize them or make them stop altogether but have a very difficult time getting off of this negative emotional merry-go-round. This happens for a few reasons. First, remember that negativity bias (where the bad stuff always gets the headline) is at play. Your lack of a relationship, lover, companion, and friend is flashing like a neon vacancy sign. You are grieving and focused on the loss, so you can expect your busy brain to look for more. Then the confirmation bias does its stuff, finding evidence to prove that you should feel sad, angry, or just plain miserable, instead of looking for (or filtering out) any data that you are okay or potentially happy. Between the external and internal triggers in your daily life, the negativity and confirmation biases keep these feelings front and center. When you are in this vicious cycle, it can seem like you are addicted to thinking about your ex and/or feeling miserable.

The one last potential contributor here may be a little hard to hear. Usually when we are in a negative pattern, there is some hidden or less obvious benefit that is serving you in some way. In Part 1, I shared how blaming my ex let me feel like a victim. You might ask how on earth feeling like a victim could be something anyone would want? The answer is that being a victim isn't what anyone wants directly, but there are some indirect or secondary benefits.

 A secondary gain is an advantage that comes from having a problem or illness. Advantages may include extra attention, sympathy, avoidance of work. The gains typically come from others' reactions to the problem, but they can unconsciously create resistance to treatment and therefore prolong the problem.

If it feels good to get sympathy from others, or to feel sorry for yourself, or keep the attention on blaming your ex instead of dealing with your own responsibility, then being the victim feels like a win. I know it sounds crazy because it doesn't seem to be a trade-off anyone would make logically. However, these trade-offs are often very subtle, and it is entirely possible that you are doing it unconsciously.

Now we know the actual science behind why we seem trapped in these negative thoughts and feelings, but it doesn't make it better. In addition, while you are stuck in pain, feeling bad every day, you are postponing the fun and happiness of meeting your new partner and starting that great relationship just ahead of you. So, let's look at some practical ways to move the process along more quickly and in a healthy way. You'll probably need to do some brutally honest soul searching if you want to heal as quickly and thoroughly as possible, but the payoff is getting out of the misery of the breakup and not going back.

Why Do You Need to Process?

Most people don't *want* to process their emotions because it involves experiencing the pain, and most people will do anything to avoid the pain. There are several very good reasons to process negative emotions. First, when you start to process your emotions, you can expect immediate relief (at least some degree). Processing emotions takes away the energetic "charge" or the intensity of the negative thoughts and resulting feelings. In a sense, processing deactivates the anxiety associated with the negative thought and emotion. Once the emotion is fully processed, you can expect to be able to have a negative thought but without the negative *feeling*. The good news is that this deactivation begins immediately.

> "that mindset of being afraid of … or avoiding negative emotions, like sadness, anger, anxiety, is actually associated with greater unhappiness. And there seems to be … something paradoxical about that, in that we and others have found that people who accept their negative emotions are actually more likely to feel better momentarily and also to say that they have a happy life in the longer term. And what we think is going on is that … if you accept your negative feelings, it

helps you to cycle through them, to work through them more quickly." (Mauss, 2017).

Second, by processing the emotion, and therefore lowering the anxiety, we can think more clearly and rationally, therefore making better decisions about how to move forward in your life.

A third reason is related to the dysfunctional ways many people cope with their pain, sadness, or anger. Chapter 9 described some of the challenges related to behaviors like emotional eating, excessive drinking or drugs, binge shopping or television watching, serial dating, etc. These behaviors can dull the pain of the negative feelings and distract you for a while. Engaging in these types of activities can offer immediate relief when you are in intense pain and may not be too harmful in moderation. However, these behaviors can also make your life worse by piling on new and different problems (e.g., gaining weight, hangovers, poor decisions under the influence, drunk driving, unprotected sex, isolation, etc.). The short-term gain of relieving our sadness momentarily is likely not worth the trouble we experience down the road. Finally, the feeling is still there. You've dulled the pain temporarily, but it will be back and even stronger next time, so you'll still have to deal with it.

The emotions don't go away; you'll eventually pay, but after inflicting even more pain by waiting. Your negative emotions get stored in the cells of your body—the mind-body connection. This means that they stay with you until they are released at a cellular level. Here is how it works.

At some point, the ignored or suppressed emotions will rear their ugly heads to find ways to get your attention. They want resolution. Periodically, when they get triggered, often unexpectedly by something minor (e.g., a song, a fear, a place, a conflict, a smell, etc.), our brains reactivate the emotion by making a connection between the current and prior situation. Each time the restimulation occurs, the emotion is reinforced through our brain's neural pathways and becomes stronger. This means you are destined to experience the emotion of the past repeatedly throughout your lifetime.

Have you ever noticed that when you're hungry, you feel the pangs of hunger for about five minutes, but then they subside for a short time (ten minutes or so)? Then the hunger comes back. This time with more intensity, but again for a short time, repeating the same pattern over again until you eat. Emotions work similarly. You can quiet the emotion temporarily, but it will return. Our genius bodies have ways to get our attention. It calls you back to take care of business (hunger and the pain of unresolved emotion).

Unresolved emotions can even lead to illness. Many studies have shown that chronic exposure to stress, anxiety, and negative moods can affect physical health in a significant way. For example, anger and hostility are related to heart disease (Chida & Steptoe, 2009), and emotional repression is linked to decreased immune system function (Bhattacharya, 2003) and cardiovascular system suppression (Simon-Thomas, 2017). Again, another way the body tries to get our attention.

Unlike hunger, emotions can be quieted for longer periods of time and can almost seem to be shut down (or controlled). Don't be fooled. The emotions will come back! They may seem to be buried deeply inside because you've become very skilled at pushing them down, but they are like a boiling tea kettle. At some point, they will blow. It will feel like the eruption is on autopilot, out of your conscious control. These unleashed emotions create great stress, and your body responds in fight-flight mode, which limits your rational thinking and ability to filter your words and actions. This is often why some people have angry outbursts or exhibit irrational obsessive fears that seem out of character. People use words or take actions they would almost never say or do under normal conditions.

For example, you could be out with friends and perceive a slight form of rejection, a simple social mistake, quite possibly what might be seen as a minor misunderstanding to most people. However, if you are harboring an intense feeling of rejection based on unresolved feelings from the breakup (or even further back in your life) and have buried this feeling deep inside, it may continue to rear its head in an ugly or insecure way. Because it's been buried for so long, it may cause you to overreact to the unintentional slight. Your efforts to keep the feelings down may fail, and unfortunately, whoever is around or inadvertently triggers the eruption will be a casualty. You've probably seen people explode in anger, fall into a deep level of depression, or go on a destructive drinking binge over some things that seem relatively small or harmless. After the feeling comes out in an intense way, the person needs to do even more to push it back down. So, the numbing behavior has to become more intense too.

It is also important to understand that some of the negative feelings (e.g., anger, rejection, shame, helplessness, fear) may have actually gotten stored in your body based on earlier negative experiences long before the relationship ended. The end of the relationship may have actually retriggered unresolved emotion from an earlier experience. For example, the pain from the end of this relationship may have triggered unresolved feelings from previous breakups.

In fact, some unsettled feelings may have started long ago when we were children and had very unsophisticated coping mechanisms. If the feelings were not processed when we first experienced them, they continue to haunt us each time they become reactivated. For example, a child who feels "left out" by other kids on the playground or always got picked last to be on the team could carry that feeling of being unwanted into their relationships as an adult.

This negative belief may be operating at the unconscious level but can sabotage you and ruin your hope of a happy long-term relationship in the future. That feeling can get triggered over and over again throughout life, with more intensity and more effort needed to quiet or stuff it down following each recurrence. And of course, most of us go to great lengths to avoid feeling the negative emotions.

In the book titled *The Untethered Soul* (Singer, 2006) there's a powerful analogy about a man who gets a thorn lodged in his arm that is directly touching the nerve. A story based on this analogy is provided to make several important points (with the author's permission).

One day a great and powerful lioness was doing just what lions are meant to do: she chased and trapped a very large zebra for dinner. But on this particular day, the lioness got much more than she bargained for because during the chase, they ran through a thicket of thorny bushes. The lioness inadvertently stepped on a branch and now had a very large thorn lodged in her paw. In the moment, the lioness was so focused on the chase that she hardly noticed the pain, but in the aftermath, she experienced extreme discomfort. She tried rubbing the paw in the grass, soaked it at the watering hole, pounded it against a tree, but nothing helped.

The thorn was right between the pads on her paw, where she could not reach it. The more she tried to relieve the pain, the deeper the thorn went and the worse the pain got. The lioness limped in pain for weeks, but over time she learned to protect the problematic paw. She even adapted by finding a different way to walk that minimized the pain.

However, she couldn't avoid triggering the pain from the thorn altogether. Occasionally, she stepped on it a certain way or brushed against something else that recreated the excruciating pain. Worst yet, sometimes another lion in the pride or one of her cubs accidentally bumped into her paw, which also set off the pain. When this happened, the lioness understandably roared ferociously and struck back reflexively with a vengeance.

Once activated, the agonizing pain could last for days and impacted her ability to track and capture her prey as well as protect herself and her cubs from other predators. Protecting the paw was a matter of life and death—it was a key to her survival. She learned from the situations that reactivated the pain and tried her very best to avoid any terrain or situations that had even the slightest chance of triggering the pain.

She became so protective that she began to anticipate potential dangers and threats in all situations (even where threats didn't exist). The lioness's hypervigilance and focus on avoiding potential pain created other problems. It limited her ability to hunt, rest, and play like the other lions in the pride. Her survival instinct and focus on protecting the paw sometimes caused her to strike out pre-emptively, so they wouldn't come near her.

*The other lions did not understand why the lioness was acting this way. They didn't understand her **seemingly** erratic and inexplicable roaring and attacking behavior. Over time, the other lions in the pride steered clear of her because they wanted to avoid being attacked. The lioness became very lonely. She unintentionally pushed the other lions away. What is most unfortunate is that the lion was simply a victim of a thorn and reacted in a very rational way, but her reactions kept the lioness from being a happy, healthy, productive member of the pride.*

This story of the lioness's *physical* pain has some parallels with what happens to us as humans when we suffer from **emotional** pain. Our emotional injuries can leave thorns in our hearts that seem unreachable and may fester when triggered by people, losses, and life events, causing similar types of undesired reactions. Emotional pain that goes unchecked can haunt us in really harmful (and sometimes unknown) ways for the rest of our lives. Not only can we miss out on the best parts of life, but the pain can get triggered over and over in life causing all sorts of havoc in repeating patterns.

Pulling out the metaphorical thorn seems like such an obvious solution, but it is far from how we typically deal with painful emotions in our lives. If we get hurt, suffer a loss, feel disappointed, we should process those feelings and move on (pulling out the thorn). Yet how many of us are willing to deal with those feelings? Most people are either unwilling or don't know how to constructively manage these emotions. We may avoid situations, people, and experiences that are important for our well-being and would actually be enjoyable and helpful if we were able to partake.

Many of the things we do to protect ourselves from experiencing and processing our emotions end up causing much more pain and difficulty in our lives. Just like the lioness from the story, who built "walls" to protect her wound and inadvertently pushed the pride away, some of the things we do in the name of protection do more harm than good. Even the smartest, most capable humans may not be aware of these "stuffed" emotions or the aftermath of their existence. Being intelligent is not the same as being emotionally self-aware.

Here is another example of how these unresolved emotions can damage new or existing relationships. Some people refer to their cautious/fearful reactions to some people or situations as setting off their "spidey sense." This gives the reaction a sense of legitimacy (i.e., infallible intuition). However, what people may actually be sensing is really just an emotional reaction from a previous hurt that was never resolved and has been reinforced over and over (e.g., the confirmation bias). Consider that the uncomfortable interaction with someone may simply be triggering the memory or pain of the previous experience with someone else from your past.

Here is an example of how this might play out. Let's say that you've been through a painful divorce and you have some unresolved feelings of rejection. Now when you are dating, if a potential partner says or does something that makes you think they might be rejecting you, you save yourself the pain of their rejection by rejecting them first. In reality, what your "spidey sense" may have picked up on was your date's healthy sense of independence. However, you may be so fearful of rejection, that even the slightest hint of it, sends you into a full-metal gear protective position. You may break off the relationship based on some misinterpreted fact. You may be totally unaware any of this is happening. This may be a repeating pattern getting in the way of your desire to be in a long-term relationship.

Your hypersensitivity may actually be a bias that clouds your judgment about what is happening in the moment. This is not to say that you shouldn't trust your intuition, particularly if your physical safety is at stake. But if you are not in harm's way, you have an opportunity to ask some questions about whether this is intuition or unresolved hurt? Have you ever felt like this before or encountered a similar situation? Could you be having an overreaction to the situation you are in based on a previous injury?

It is also interesting to consider that there is work involved in either path, process or ignore the emotions. Yes, processing emotions takes time, patience, some effort, and yes, it will hurt temporarily. But as you know from your own life experience, it takes a lot of work to avoid feelings too. Unfortunately, we too often take the more painful path of avoiding feelings which adds insult to the injury in many ways. Basically, it comes down to a question: Do you want to handle it now or later when the costs are higher? There is great value in processing emotional pain. I believe it is our only chance of being free and fully alive. In fact, if you don't, you are never really fully living.

In summary, there are basically two options when it comes to our negative feelings. The broad categories can be described as embracing your feelings or pushing them away. As I described previously, you can shove the feelings down by ignoring them, pretending they don't exist, distracting or numbing yourself (e.g., using alcohol, drugs, sex, shopping, gambling, overeating, etc.). The cost of this path is too high. In addition, it doesn't solve anything because the emotions still need to be processed and are just waiting for the next time your guard is down, so they can rear their ugly head to get your attention.

It's a lousy option, so let's move on to the next chapter that focuses on the work of processing emotional pain and moving on to get the great relationship you want.

Getting It Right

- The end of your relationship gives you an opportunity to understand your emotions and manage them in a new, healthier way.
- A breakup typically triggers painful thoughts and emotions. The negativity and confirmation biases kick in and can keep you stuck on a negative merry-go-round.
- Processing your emotions relieves your pain and brings you more joy and helps you move on. This will not only improve your love life but will enhance all aspects of your life.

- Many people are not aware of their emotions, understand their importance, or how to manage them. They are also in the dark about the consequences of avoiding their feelings.

- In addition, as humans it's natural to fight and avoid feeling these emotions, often with a ferocious intensity. Unfortunately, this approach has serious implications.

- Emotions can be temporarily quieted but never shut down completely—they will come back, often in intense, destructive, or explosive ways.

- Research shows there's a connection between repressed emotions and poor health. If you ignore or avoid your emotions, you'll likely experience more serious negative consequences down the road.

- Numbing, pushing away, or postponing dealing with painful emotions takes more work than processing them. These diversions are ultimately more painful than just doing the processing work in the first place. It's really a matter of paying now or paying later. You will pay eventually, often when the costs are higher.

- There is great value in processing emotional pain. It deactivates the anxiety and intensity of the emotions and allows you to move forward free from the anger, sadness, fear, or hurt. When you do, you'll find a new way of fully living.

Chapter Eleven:

Diffusing Negative Emotions

Congratulations, you are about to embark on one of the most important and life-changing journeys of your life! Just by reading this chapter, you will become more aware of your emotions and take your first steps forward toward better emotional health. Even if you are an expert in managing emotions, the breakup offers a significant opportunity to check in on unresolved emotional pain. It is a very exciting and worthwhile effort with great rewards.

People vary greatly in their knowledge, comfort, and skill in managing their emotions. If you are new to emotions, don't have a lot of information, or are uncomfortable dealing with your painful negative emotions, it may be helpful to start with some basics.

Tips for getting in touch with your emotions:

Grow Your Emotional Vocabulary: If you are unfamiliar with feelings, it can be very helpful to grow your emotional vocabulary. Research on emotions suggests that people who have a well-developed emotional vocabulary are better at managing their emotions. Get to know more feeling words and their definitions. Examples of emotional vocabulary lists are provided in the Resources section. Try to incorporate more of these in your everyday conversation (and thinking).

Recognize the progressive nature of emotions: Many lists of emotional vocabulary words categorize them (e.g., happiness, anger, fear, etc.) and then detail a progression based on the intensity of the feeling. For example, in the category of happiness with strong intensity, we find words like elated, vibrant, delighted, or exhilarated. In the same category but with less intensity: contented, pleased, satisfied. In describing depression, you might use bleak or hopeless for strong intensity of feeling vs. blah or subdued when the intensity is less.

Identify your Feelings: Ask yourself how you feel *right now*. Then be patient. There's a learning curve to naming your feelings. Give yourself a few minutes to identify a feeling. Use the emotions list to see if anything on the list resonates. Ask the question more frequently until you become more aware of your feelings.

Identify a Physical Component (if possible): There's a connection between our minds and our bodies. Remember unresolved emotions are stored in your body. You may recognize some bodily clues about your feelings or vice versa. For example, you may be upset about an argument with a friend and then notice a tight feeling in your chest. Alternatively, you might have a splitting headache and then determine it is related to the stress you've been under. You may even be able to point the onset of the headache back to some stressful situation that occurred during the day. Check in with your body to see if it can give you some clues about your feelings.

Be Patient: You might have a little trouble getting in touch with your feelings. Many people say, "I'm not feeling anything." That could mean that you are experiencing a low intensity feeling like contentment, satisfied, or even apathy. You may have also shut down your feelings, so you truly can't identify a feeling at this point. Be patient, give yourself a few quiet moments to clear your mind then ask again. You may need to come back later or start again when you are feeling a more intense emotion.

Acknowledge Confusion: If you notice confusion about your emotions, you may have conflicting emotions or multiple feelings operating at once. For example, you might have a negative emotion you don't feel safe acknowledging or maybe you feel really sad the relationship is over, but you also have a sense of relief, which makes you unsure about your conflicting feelings. If you don't know how you are feeling, it's likely due to a "bad" feeling you don't want to acknowledge.

Emotional Triggers: If you have a hard time talking about your emotions at first, try finding a song that describes your feelings or watch a drama that elicits strong feelings. Songs are a great way to express your emotion. Observe how a sad song can bring you in touch with your sad feelings really quickly. There are so many breakup songs, you shouldn't have any trouble finding several that describe your feelings. As a side note, for some people, music can help you *shift* out of your negative emotion. Try singing along to a happy song when you are down.

Include Emotions in Conversations: When you are talking with people, try using more "I" statements with feelings (e.g., "I feel frustrated, excited, confused, hurt, or afraid"). You can also ask them how they are feeling or use reflective listening to check in on how they are feeling. For example, after someone describes a tough day, you can say, "It sounds like you had a frustrating day." The more you incorporate feelings into your experience, the more skilled you will become at processing them. You'll be surprised about people's reactions, even at work. They will hardly notice you are doing this and will actually respond well when they notice your level of empathy.

There are multiple paths we can take to deal with negative emotions in a healthy way. Some methods include working with professionals, and there are several methods you can do on your own. Some methods align with traditional Western medicine and some fall under the umbrella of alternative healing—adaptations of ancient Chinese healing methods. There are no right or wrong ways to go about this. Think of this as a menu and pick the options that interest or resonate with you.

Professional Help

Many people want and need professional help to get through this crushing heartache. This is highly encouraged especially if you don't have a network of (or at least one) trusted, wise, empathetic, unbiased friends or family members to talk with on a regular basis as you go through this. (And frankly, how many people do?) If you have not sought out professional help in the past, here are a couple of suggestions to consider.

There are several types of professionals who may be able to support you through these difficult times. Helping professionals can range from psychiatrists, psychologists, social workers, licensed professional counselors, or could even be people at your church who are trained to help you.

There is no right or wrong answer here, but it's important for you to find someone you are comfortable with who will help you. It's also important that you take responsibility for getting the right person to help you.

It may not be easy to navigate the options available to you. Many people may select their providers based on who is covered by their insurance, who is closest or who can see them in the next two months (many professionals are booked out months in advance). Because there is still stigma around mental health, it may be difficult to get a referral from friends of family, but if it is possible, a good reference can be very helpful. Many organizations have a confidential employee assistance program (EAP) available to you for no charge. This might be a good way to explore getting some help without a large investment of time and money.

Your helping professional will meet with you on a regular basis (e.g., weekly, bi-weekly or monthly). Their therapy will likely include collecting a comprehensive history and inventory of your life, including your concerns, current issues, and living conditions. They use this information to support an accurate diagnosis and identify the best treatment approach. In your sessions, your therapist will typically ask questions, listen, help you uncover your beliefs, gently challenge them (when appropriate), act as a sounding board, and can help provide a balanced perspective. A typical form of treatment that aligns well with the information provided in this book is called Cognitive, Behavior Therapy.

Cognitive Behavioral Therapy: A particularly effective technique that focuses on learning to cope with less helpful thinking and behavior patterns. In general, it recognizes that your problems are based on limiting thoughts and beliefs, and helps people recognize those faulty patterns, face their fears, and develop better coping skills.

Alternative Medicine – Energy Healing

Another type of healing comes from an emerging field of alternative medicine practitioners. Many fall under the umbrella of energy healers and have a variety of methods and practices to support the removal of blocked energy that results when you have trapped negative emotions. Examples include Reiki, acupuncture, emotional freedom techniques (EFT), energy medicine, etc. Some practitioners leverage a hybrid approach combining the use of traditional therapies with alternative medicine. The Resources section at the back of the book provides some links that may help you find practioners in your area.

As a young adult, I had multiple reasons to seek help from mental health professionals including close family members and friends dealing with alcoholism, suicide attempts, and sexual abuse. I learned later that my family of origin had a long history of mental illness. On a more personal level, I was an emotional eater most of my life and I got married at a very young age to a wonderful man who also came from a dysfunctional family. Needless to say, we had loads of issues. I was hungry for a better way to live and be happy. In my lifetime, I have worked with no fewer than eight psychologists, many of whom I liked and called friends after the therapy ended. Looking back, I know it was helpful, but I was searching for some kind of help that would be more efficient and effective.

*As I became more of an educated consumer in the mental health arena, I was looking for a better way. I remember the day I did a search for alternative medicine in my area. I found three physicians and one mental health provider. The mental health provider was a psychologist but also used different methods of energy healing (see Dr. Erin Shannon's website in Resources). I called that day and made my first appointment. Now I am a **huge** advocate of alternative medicine, and in particular energy medicine (see the section later in this chapter). She not only helped me but taught me how to help myself. The methods I learned were extremely effective. My life is completely transformed, and it happened relatively quickly. After years of mainstream psychotherapy, in my experience, there is just no comparison to the speed and effectiveness of energy medicine and the other alternative medicine methods I learned.*

Self-Administered Methods of Processing Emotions

Journaling

Much has been written about the benefits of journaling—actually putting pen to paper to record your thoughts. The greatest benefit may come from focusing on ourselves for a few quiet minutes without distraction. You can journal in an unstructured way, but it can also be helpful to answer relevant questions. The key questions for you might include an exploration of your prior thoughts and feelings about the relationship before it ended. Get curious about your thoughts about the relationship before it ended, maybe for months prior to the breakup. Put your memory to work as these thoughts impacted how you showed up in the relationship, for better or for worse. You definitely want to explore your feelings. It's also good to spend time on your current thoughts and expectations, hopes, and fears. There is a good list of questions to help you unpack your emotions in the Appendix at the end of the book.

Feel Your Feelings (FYF)

The first and easiest way to process your emotions is to feel the feelings. This technique could be described as an emotional self-awareness and letting go experience. We try to avoid the pain because it is uncomfortable, but if we allow ourselves to feel it (even for a relatively short period of time), we can get rid of it for good. If you can permit the pain, instead of pushing it away, you can end the pain vs. reactivating it every time you encounter a situation that re-stimulates the feeling. Allowing the feeling to come out and accepting it temporarily is a way to validate yourself and validate the feeling in a way that takes the "charge" or energy out of the feeling.

Think of it this way: You had a traumatic experience, and it caused a lot of pain, fear, anger, etc., but you won't acknowledge the trauma or the painful feeling. It's as if you tell the feeling, "You aren't real, you don't exist or have a right to be in my life. I don't want you and will do everything in my power to deny you." The feeling is screaming, "OMG… will you please just notice me? I'm real; you were injured, and it hurts. I'm not going away until you know I exist and acknowledge me." If you choose to acknowledge and feel the feeling for a while, this will satisfy and validate the feeling so the intensity will subside.

What exactly does it look like or mean to feel your feelings? The first step is to identify the feeling. Do you know what you are feeling? You may not know. You may only be aware that you are uncomfortable, unhappy, or anxious. We have to be quiet and still sometimes to get in touch with a feeling. You'll need to slow down, take some deep breaths, and ask yourself what feeling is present. Refer back to the tips on getting in touch with your emotions at the beginning of this chapter (e.g., look at a list of emotions to see if any of them fit with your experience).

This is not a time to be in your thoughts. What you are thinking and feeling are not the same. You may be conscious of a thought but try to also get curious about the emotion attached. For example, you might think that your ex-boyfriend left you after years of being together, and his words promising he loved you and wanted to get married were misleading.

Next ask how you feel about that? Perhaps anger resonates. You may be able to go a little deeper and see if there is another emotion that also describes what you are feeling in a more specific way (e.g., betrayed, disappointed, hopeless about finding another partner, regret over giving him so many years). In addition, try to move beyond the primary emotions (e.g., happy, sad, angry, afraid), and get down to another level. For example, underneath anger there are many different levels. Are you frustrated, irritated, furious, or livid? There's no need to explain the feeling at this step. Identifying it is all that is required.

Don't be too hard on yourself if you can't quite identify the feeling. You may unintentionally confuse your emotions with your thoughts. It's okay to have thoughts about situations, but then ask how you are *feeling* about that thought. Be patient with yourself. Try to accept your feelings whatever they are. You may have to come back to it later. This is not something you learn overnight. It's like learning a new skill and may take time. Be patient with yourself.

Remember the tip earlier to look for a connection between the mind and the body. Some people find it helpful to identify where the emotion resides in their body. For example, as you name the emotion do you notice tension in your chest or neck, an upset stomach, or even back pain?

The next step is to allow yourself the time and space to feel the feeling. Sit quietly with the feeling. Let the emotion wash over you, wallow in it; let it take you over. This is not the time for thinking, problem solving, judgment, blaming, etc. Yes, I do know very well that this is difficult. But it is also so worth the effort and discomfort. Hang in there. No pain, no gain. It will not take long to pass. Don't be surprised if you cry. Don't be surprised if you don't cry. There is no right or wrong here. Just allow yourself time to do nothing but feel the feeling. While you are feeling the feeling, try to breathe deeply and slowly. As you are allowing yourself to experience your emotions, practice brutal self-acceptance and self-care. Treat yourself with as much kindness and compassion as you would for someone else you love who is experiencing their difficult feelings.

BRFWA: My friend and yoga teacher offered the following tip as a way to remember how to work through and release emotions: Breath, relax, feel, watch, and allow—BRFWA.

When you sense that the intensity or "charge" of the feeling has subsided, you will begin to feel less anxious, calmer, and the "charge" or intensity of the emotion will be lower. You will sense when the anxiety of the feeling subsides—you'll feel more centered and at peace. It doesn't mean you won't still hurt, but it will hurt much less. If you still hurt, follow the process again.

Congratulations... you have just "processed" an emotion. When you have finished FYF, you may have some thoughts or new insights about your situation. This is a great place to do some journaling. You'll find you are in a much better position to think rationally and clearly. If you noticed some bodily sensations earlier (e.g., a headache or tension in your neck), you may also want to observe if there has been a change in the sensation. Don't be alarmed if you don't have this experience; it's really a matter of extra credit.

Depending on size and scale of the emotion, this may need to be repeated several times, but for now it may be best to walk away and come back at another time.

Feel Your Feeling Then Let Go (FYF-LG)

This second method is an adaptation of a technique based on the Sedona method (see Resources) and is very similar to the first approach—FYFs. However, there are a couple of additional steps. Basically, after you identify (name) the emotion, ask yourself three questions:

1) Can I feel the feeling? Will I sit quietly and allow myself to feel the pain of the emotion without pushing it away?
2) Can I let it go? Is it possible to intentionally make a decision to let it go?
3) Will I let it go? Am I willing to let it go?

Take each question individually, giving yourself time to process each with a few minutes in between to take some breaths and clear your mind. Sometimes you might need to repeat the cycle multiple times, now or later.

For question #1 if the answer is yes, then follow the instructions for FYF as previously described. Allow the feeling to wash over you. Stay with it. Just be with the feeling; try not to think.

If the answer to question #1 is no, that's okay. Here are some tips to help you answer yes at some point down the road.

1. Ask yourself what is needed to help you feel the emotion? Some of the information in the FYF instructions on identifying and naming the feeling may be helpful to consider with this question.

2. It could also be helpful to think about the consequences of ignoring negative feelings that were also outlined earlier when we covered why you need to process. You can ask, "What is the worst thing that can happen if I let myself feel this feeling? What exactly am I afraid of?" Sometimes confronting the

worst thing and then recognizing it isn't so bad allows us to be more willing. Most people can get to a place where they will be able to answer yes in time; until then, practice compassion and understanding with yourself.

3. It can also be helpful to internally express a desire to feel and learn to process the emotion. Allow the intention to be your focus for now; let that be enough until you are ready.

For question #2, ask yourself if you are ready to let it go or if you need to hold on longer. ***This question includes a recognition that we have power over our thoughts and decisions.*** Sometimes it feels as if we are hostage to our sadness and anger, but that isn't true. We can decide to let the feelings go whenever we choose. If the answer is yes, then have an internal discussion about the benefits of letting go and move onto question #3.

If the answer is no, you may be in a spot where you intellectually want to let the feeling go but are not ready to do so. If this is the case, then accept that this is where you are and let it be a good awareness that you have an opportunity for additional healing down the road. It may be very helpful to consider the secondary gains that come from emotions we don't like. For example, remember the discussion on the secondary benefits of being a victim? You may be choosing to play the victim because of the sympathy and attention you get, even though you may not want to continue feeling weak and helpless overall.

A second explanation for why you can't say yes to question #2 is that you don't believe it's possible to let go of the feeling. Can you think of times in your life when you were able to let go of painful emotions? For example, were you ever able to forgive and forget in the past when someone hurt you before? This is the same thing. Maybe there were different circumstances, but the fact that you have been able to do it before shows that you are dealing with choices. You could trust in the process and give it a try.

Or you may still need more evidence to prove this to yourself. You can start by experimenting with simpler emotions in smaller stakes situations. For example, did you have a difference of opinion with someone at work? Work through question #1 and see if you can get through questions #2 and #3. Make a decision to let go, believe it is possible, and watch what happens. Next try it with other negative emotions and see if it gets easier. By the way, this process of experimentation and testing the results is a good way to change your beliefs. When you experience multiple small wins about your ability to process an emotion, you fundamentally change your beliefs about your capability to process emotions. When you can believe that feelings can be let go, then you can answer yes to question #2 and make the decision to do so.

If the answer in question #3 (Am I willing to let it go?) is yes, then have an internal dialogue to release the emotion. As human beings, we want to be thought of as reliable people. Research shows that we are motivated to be consistent between what we think, what we say, and what we do. This is described in behavioral science as the commitment or consistency bias. As brain biases go, this one can actually work in your favor if you want to make a positive change.

Commitment and consistency bias: a tendency to continue to act according to the previous actions and commitments we've made. It's a reluctance to change our course of action once we've chosen it.

Because inconsistency is perceived negatively, people try harder to keep their promises and show consistency in their words and actions. You can leverage this to process your emotions more effectively. For example, since we are more likely to follow through with something if we say we are going to do it, saying, "I'm willing to let this go" internally or out loud makes it more powerful. If we write it down or say publicly, there's an even stronger chance we'll do it.

You can also use techniques such as visualization to "see" yourself letting go. Or write down the emotion you want to let go of on a piece of paper and then burn it or tear it up to help you let the emotion go.

Not all emotional reactions are created equal; some are more intense, more personal, and more sensitive than others. Feel free to try different methods to find out what works best for you to really let it go. As is the case with FYFs, there are no right or wrongs with trying and practicing this method. You may need to rinse and repeat depending on the intensity and history of the emotion (e.g., if it goes back to childhood). You may be able to repeat the cycle in one sitting until you no longer feel the "charge" of the emotion (e.g., it no longer makes you feel angry or need to cry) or may need to come back at a later time and repeat the process again.

While both of the processes described above seem incredibly simple, I have found great success with them personally and with many people I have introduced them to. If you are like me, you might be scratching your head wondering, "Why do we work so hard to stuff down our feelings when it seems so simple to process them?" I don't have the answer, but I can tell you that after having hundreds of positive experiences processing negative emotions, I still find myself reluctant at times. I believe it is just part of our human nature to resist pain, but it's a lot easier to process your emotions more quickly and easily with more practice.

When to Process

Now that you've learned more about a couple of ways to process your emotions, here are some ideas to help set you up for success. First is to find a quiet place and time to do the processing. Then decide when you are going to process.

<u>Processing Later</u>

The processing techniques outlined above can be incredibly helpful in all types of situations for simple or more complex and/or stronger emotional reactions as well. These techniques can be used ***after*** you have an upsetting experience or loss, either immediately after or if you aren't in a position to process the emotion at that moment, you can still use them to process the emotion later. Remember our unprocessed emotions don't go away, so you can access them later to restimulate the emotion and resolve it. Frankly, it doesn't matter if the emotions are buried from years and years ago. They can still be accessed, processed, and released to create a healthier life.

In the Moment

With practice, these methods can also be helpful processing emotions in the moment, during the triggering situation (e.g., a confrontation with your ex, your children, or someone at work). When you begin to recognize an emotional reaction during the disagreement, you can choose to feel the emotion, name it, allow it into your experience, and decide to let it go in the moment. This helps you deal more effectively with more rational judgment and problem solving for whatever the argument happens to be about.

Of course, this is more difficult to do when you are having a more intense reaction or when it does not feel safe to express your feelings publicly (e.g., crying at work). In addition, you just may not have the time or ability to put your full attention on processing the feeling in the moment. In these cases, it's okay to acknowledge the feeling (name it internally and recognize its existence) and the inability to fully process it now. Look for the next time you can be alone to safely process the emotion. ***The sooner you can take time to do the processing work, the better.*** Be aware that since we have a natural human tendency to avoid pain, don't wait too long!

Once you become practiced, it can be fast and easy to process your emotions and hardly miss a beat. Processing in the moment allows you to function at a higher level and make better decisions. When you process your emotions, you are able to think clearly rather than potentially making an inappropriate comment in the heat of the moment. For example, I've worked with several people who have learned these approaches during work meetings with great success!

One other thing worth mentioning is that having a memory about your relationship or a negative thought or feeling about your ex (even though it's about the past) is a form of a triggering event in the moment. Processing the emotion of the memory or thought as quickly as possible is ideal.

As mentioned earlier, I've become an advocate of energy healing because I found it so beneficial personally. Therefore, information and resources about these alternative medicine methods are provided in the hope that you might benefit too. In fairness, there is controversy about the scientific evidence and effectiveness for energy healing. However, there are many areas of science and medicine that are still emerging and not yet well understood or accepted (e.g., emotions, disease, viruses/vaccines, mental illness, etc.). In addition, many new discoveries take years, and often require a paradigm shift before gaining acceptance by the medical community. Just like everything else in this book, think of it like a menu. Take what you like and leave the rest.

Energy Healing

Energy healing combines concepts and procedures from ancient Eastern healing traditions with contemporary science and practices to provide a holistic approach to health and wellness. It relies on the understanding of the mind-body connection and emphasizes self-healing. It can address both physical and emotional issues.

Energy healing (also known as energy medicine) allows you to heal your body by activating your body's energies and by restoring the energies that have become weak, blocked, or out of balance.

When situations arise in which we feel threatened, and the emotions are not addressed, energy becomes trapped. These blockages occur and accumulate over a lifetime. The emotional impact of trauma (e.g., being in a car accident, observing physical abuse, or a fire in the home) is obvious, but smaller traumas such as minor offenses, arguments, or misunderstandings occur much more frequently and can also leave unresolved emotions that block energies

For example, most people have experiences from their childhood when they were upset about something. They could have been scolded by a teacher, had a fight with a brother or sister, or maybe got separated from a parent while shopping and were lost. These relatively small experiences (little traumas) also created emotions that may not have been resolved and released. These are examples of trapped emotions which are stored in the cells of the body and are carried forward into adulthood. When difficult emotions like anger, fear, resentment, guilt, and sadness are not processed, they block the flow of positive energy in our bodies. Energy healing simply helps to remove the trapped emotions.

Emotional Freedom Technique (EFT)

One of the fastest and most effective ways to process emotions and accelerate the healing process is through a process called Emotional Freedom Technique (EFT). It's a mind-body approach designed to release energy blocked in the body's energy system due to these stuck emotions. EFT disrupts or breaks up the blockage and neutralizes the negative impact. While it may sound unconventional, it is amazingly effective, fast, adaptable to many situations, easy to learn, risk free, and costs nothing.

How It Works

EFT is also known as Tapping because during the process you tap on some acupressure points while you think about what's bothering you. Recognizing the connection between the mind and the body, it simultaneously involves both. When thinking about an issue that raises negative emotion (e.g., fear, sadness, anger, shame, etc.), the restimulation of that emotion triggers the fight-flight response. This makes it more difficult to objectively process the emotion. The action of tapping on the prescribed acupressure points calms the body's fight-flight stress reaction, which allows you to more rationally manage it.

EFT is considered a form of alternative medicine and is not yet widely accepted in Western medicine. However, there is a mounting body of scientific research supporting its effectiveness. To date, there have been 84 published studies in peer-reviewed journals (which means they were reviewed by other experts in the field before being published, which suggests higher scientific rigor). The majority of the studies found that EFT led to positive results. In addition, three separate meta-analyses (a statistical procedure in which data from multiple studies are combined) were conducted to synthesize the data across studies of energy medicine. In all three, EFT was effective in treating anxiety, depression, and PTSD with large effect sizes—the measurement of the strength of a relationship (Clond, M., 2016, Sebastian, B., & Nelms, J., 2017, Mavranezouli, I. et al., 2019). As is the case with many innovations, large paradigm shifts take time.

While EFT has some good scientific evidence, it is still lagging in the mainstream acceptance and use. However, there are plenty of good reasons to give it a try.

More Specifics on EFT

In the EFT process, people call to mind their painful issue, emotion or situation and begin tapping on specific acupressure points. The tapping points are primarily on the head and chest. The participant uses a series of verbal statements to describe the situation and how they feel about it. As was described above, people who begin to think about a painful experience or situation will trigger the pain of that situation, as if they are reliving it in the moment again to some degree. People triggered by anxiety typically struggle to think clearly, try to suppress their uncomfortable feelings, and operate under distorted judgment, etc. This was covered in Part 1.

The calming effect of the tapping on the acupressure points provides relief instead of the normal anxious stressful reaction to the painful emotions. It allows the participant to access difficult emotions and the stressful memories and thoughts of the past or their current pain in a healthier way, which allows them to process effectively and remove any energy blockages. It also allows them to be fully present with the emotions and see them for what they are in an objective way.

Without the stressful anxious reaction, the participant can work through the situation and emotions with a mindful compassionate awareness. The painful emotions are able to be fully validated, explored, and then released, which also eliminates the harmful effects of the negative emotion (see Resources for more information).

When I was first introduced to this method, I was as skeptical as they come. It seemed ridiculous to me. I've been using EFT now for years with amazing effects and have shared it with others who have also reported phenomenal results.

Emotion Code

Another energy healing technique developed to release trapped emotions is called the Emotion Code. Dr. Brad Nelson developed this process which can also be self-administered or with the help and support of a practitioner. This process relies on the mind-body connection to very simply identify trapped emotions and release them by tracing on the governing meridian (an energy path through the body). One of the benefits of the process is that while you can release painful trapped emotions from the past, it is not necessary to relive or restimulate those emotions. Like EFT, this process is remarkably quick and effective.

FAQs about Processing Emotions

As you begin to understand how you can process your emotions and the best time to do so, you may have additional questions, so let's take a look at some of these.

How long does the processing technique take?

As you get started, you'll want to give yourself the time and space to process as much as possible. The time needed to do this varies widely. However, you may be able to process a simple emotion in just a few moments (more thoroughly in five to ten minutes), but it might take 20 to 30 minutes for a more painful intense emotion. As is the case with anything new, there's always a learning curve, so add a little more time in the beginning. Another tip for beginners is to try to do this with as much time available as possible. You don't want to box yourself in and add the pressure of needing to finish at a certain time while learning to process. This is especially important if you are in heavy emotional pain.

Keep in mind that when processing emotions, other memories, thoughts, and feelings may come to the surface. Immediately after a breakup you may have a flood of emotions, so you might want to sit with them for up to an hour at a time. But in my experience, 40 minutes is about as much time as I've ever needed. When you consider the havoc these unresolved feelings cause in our lives, spending this amount of time seems like a no brainer.

How long does the overall healing process take?

If you are like me, you've heard people say, "For every year you were together, it takes a month to heal." Unfortunately, for many long-term relationships, this may be more of the norm than the exception. While this has been the case for many people, it doesn't need to be the case for you. The good news is that the work of processing your emotions can accelerate the healing process immensely. You are in control of how long it takes to be in a healthy place. It doesn't have to continue for weeks or months or years.

How much time it actually takes depends on the severity of the pain, your comfort or experience dealing with your emotions, and your desire to tackle the processing work. However, it won't happen overnight. Whatever caused the breakup didn't start overnight. There may have been a triggering event that appears to have caused the breakup, but there was most likely an underlying issue that was building over time. The underlying issue may not be apparent until you begin the processing the relationship (Helpful Thoughts, Chapter 8) and your emotions.

A big determinant of the time needed will be your tolerance for pain and your tendency to avoid and numb the discomfort. The processing work involves an internal discovery journey. Believe it or not, you have all the answers inside. However, much of what we need to learn may be elusive and will take some quiet reflection time to discover.

Processing our emotions allows us to reduce the anxiety and natural tendency to push difficult thoughts and emotions away. Therefore, we are able to uncover the issues that were unreachable before and do so in a much faster way. As was discussed earlier, often our pain today is attached or connected to prior hurts. If the earlier hurts weren't thoroughly processed, our new situation may be irritating the older painful feelings (remember the lioness and the thorn). We need to get down to the root level removing as many of the core feelings as possible. Yes, this can be difficult. The promise though is that if you work through the processing, you will be able to get what you want in the next relationship. Without it, there's a good likelihood the painful patterns will repeat themselves.

Recently while processing an emotion, I was able to trace it back to two experiences from my childhood when I struggled with people "not liking me." These were not significant traumatic experiences but simple examples of daily life where I observed that a couple of people (a camp counselor and a neighbor) didn't seem to like me. One was valid and the other was actually a false impression. However seemingly insignificant, my young brain (5 or 6 years old) didn't have a great way to process these experiences or feelings. I believe I walked away with a strong sense of wanting people to like me and being unhappy when they didn't.

While I remembered these experiences and could understand my childhood misperception of the situation, I realized there may have been a more harmful impact because, as an adult, I continued to be overly sensitive to people who were unhappy with me. I eventually realized I hadn't gotten in touch with or felt the sadness of the perceived rejection. I think I was intellectualizing the situation instead of feeling it, and therefore it continued to plague me.

But in this one moment as a mature adult, I was able to feel the sadness of being turned away by a playmate and overhearing a camp counselor say she didn't like me. Honestly, it was NOT an awful, overwhelming sadness. Instead, I felt a joyful release after letting it out. I was also relieved to know it would no longer have a hold on me.

Our brains are so fascinating. Why out of a whole lifetime of experiences, did I remember these two seemingly insignificant experiences with pretty good detail (when I remember little else from being 5 or 6 years old)? I believe ***they stand out because they formed the beginning of my belief system about myself and others. In addition, my emotions were trapped in my cell memory and became stimulated repeatedly in life when I encountered people who didn't seem to like me or were unhappy with me.***

Today I recognize the ways that this small hurt over not being liked continued to torment me in many ways as a people-pleasing adult. My older and wiser adult recognizes that it's unrealistic for everyone to like me, and I'm okay when they don't. I don't need to change the way I talk, think, act, or look to be more acceptable or likable. However, there were still irrational remnants of my desire to be liked at play until I was able to release this trapped emotion. This integration of the past with the current is another effective way to complete the processing cycle.

Sometimes in order to gain the perspective needed for success, it can be helpful to go in and out of the processing work. This work can be intense and uncomfortable, so sometimes stepping away and doing smaller bits at a time can be the most productive option. Waiting a day or a week between processing sessions can give you a needed break from the effort and pain in order to come back in a more productive state. Haven't you noticed that things almost always look different in the morning or days later? Our bodies and minds have a remarkable and wonderful way of rebooting overnight.

It is important to note that giving yourself time to feel and process the emotion is not the same as wallowing in it endlessly. ***Processing is about allowing the feeling to exist, be present, and then releasing it.*** Holding on to the pain and misery, feeling sad, lonely, and sorry for ourselves for weeks, months, and years is ***not*** processing emotions. Processing your emotions will help relieve some of the immediate intensity of the pain of a breakup (even though it may not go away entirely at first, depending on the situation). If you are in a lot of emotional pain three or four months after the breakup, you likely have more processing to do. Go at it again to get to a different level; try another method; or it might be time to talk to a professional.

Getting It Right

- Making the decision to learn about and process your emotions will likely be one of the most important and significant opportunities you have to thrive and find your ideal partner.

- Remember this is a skill many people have not mastered. It may take a little time to practice, but the payoff is worth the effort.

- Exploring emotions can be quite frightening at first but try some experiments with emotions that feel safe to build your confidence. Keep in mind that the process is relatively fast and effective, once you get past the hurdles.

- There are many tips for getting started. Expanding your emotional vocabulary and increasing the use of emotional language in your conversation is a good way to get better at identifying what you're feeling.

- Processing your emotions can be done with the help of a professional or by using self-administered methods.

- In addition to traditional helping professionals (e.g., psychologists or counselors), alternative healing methods are emerging, including Reiki, acupuncture, energy medicine, and holistic well-being coaches with a good track record of success. Do not be too quick to dismiss these.

- There are good self-administered methods of processing emotions including journaling, self-awareness and letting go experiences, Emotional Freedom Technique (Tapping) and the Emotional Code.

- Processing your emotions will diffuse the pain and release blocked energy caused by unprocessed emotions. Living a life without fear of emotions can help you experience a new level of being fully alive.

Part 3: Get the Relationship You Want

Identify what you want!

Do you know what you want in your next relationship? You probably have a pretty good idea, and that's why you are excited to be reading this last section of the book—you are ready to go get it. If you do, fantastic, but keep an open mind as you read this section. You might see an opportunity to reshape how you are thinking about what you want. You may also realize that there are things that might delight you that you never even imagined!

The way you think and talk about what you want can impact your success reaching your ideal state. (More to come on this later.) If you don't know what you want, no worries. The ideas in this section can help you give it some thought and define it a little better.

It is important to define what you want. Defining what you want could come in the form of setting goals, setting intentions, and/or making a list of the characteristics, preferences and interests of your future partner. Goals and intentions have power. They can help us by looking to see what is possible, hold a shining light on our bright future, and help mobilize our thoughts and actions toward our future vision.

Chapter Twelve

Goals, Intentions, and Preferences

Goals

Goals are defined as targets for what you want to accomplish, have, or do for the future. They often have deadlines. You might commonly think of setting goals for things like successfully completing a large-scale project at work, hitting a sales target, physical challenges (increase your running speed), weight loss, or learning to speak a different language fluently. Relationship goals are a bit different. For example, you might have a goal to get married in the next two years, to be a good provider for your family (e.g., reach a certain level of financial support), or maybe you simply want to have a "plus one" for life's events and celebrations by the summer. These are all examples of relationship outcomes or "accomplishments."

There is a great deal of research on the motivational power of goals. Goals can inspire us, help us set direction and make plans (which help us think through the steps needed to achieve the goal), and may compel us into action when we feel some excitement or pressure to move forward. Goals that are aspirational, specific, and measurable are most effective. Herein lies the challenge with goals. The key is related to whether the goal makes you feel good or bad. If you can "see" yourself accomplishing the goal and are enthusiastic about getting there, then having a relationship goal is great. The positive state of excitement and enthusiasm will inspire you to take appropriate action to reach the goal.

On the other hand, if you see the gap between where you are today and where you want to be, and you are discouraged and not hopeful about your ability to reach the goal, then having the goal may actually sabotage your efforts. The feelings of frustration or despair associated with having a goal that seems unreachable can seriously deter motivation and effort.

This is true even when that frustration is operating below the radar of conscious thought. For example, if you stay positive and don't allow yourself to think or talk about failure, your fear of failure could still be a powerful force sabotaging your success. Again, ***the important indicators of your success are your feelings.***

Even the most highly motivated people may have trouble reaching relationship goals. Obviously, there are two people involved in a relationship and the other person is out of your control. When you have doubt about your ability to achieve the goal, the goal can cause anxiety, fear, and feelings of inadequacy. You may not be *aware* that you have any doubts or realize how strong or powerful they are, but it is very possible that they exist. In fact, it would be unusual if you don't have doubts because most people have had several (or maybe even a lifetime of) disappointing relationship experiences that are difficult to ignore. This prior experience is amplified due to the negativity bias (see Part 1), which also impacts your ability to find a great mate.

Alternatively, the goal may motivate you into action, but you might not take the best action when you are operating from a negative mindset. For example, if your relationship deadline is looming, you may feel desperate and take unhealthy risks you wouldn't ordinarily take or settle for a partner who isn't the best fit. These are the primary dangers with setting relationship goals. If you have negative feelings associated with the goal, your choices are to either process the emotion (see Chapter 11) or consider abandoning the goal since it may be doing more harm than good.

A final difficulty related to setting relationship goals is the potential to think small. If you've experienced many relationship challenges in your past, you may be lowering your expectations, so you won't be disappointed. Are you settling for what you think might be possible instead of setting a goal to get what you truly want? This is another potential downfall of goal setting. A better alternative is to try setting intentions.

Intentions

Intentions are different from goals. If goals provide a relationship target with specific measures, intentions deal with the quality of life and relationship you want to create. An intention is focused on how you want to live in the relationship, how you want to be or "show up" with your partner, and how it will feel (as individuals and as a couple). Examples here could include:

- We enjoy great stimulating conversations.
- We spend a lot of time together, but we also have our own space and time.
- We are very active, love events, are always learning and trying new things.
- We are surrounded by great friends and family.

- We are comfortable in non-traditional roles and support each other's preferences.
- We care about our health and share healthy practices, meals, and exercise.
- We love each other unconditionally, communicate fearlessly, and forgive easily.
- My partner loves and is a great role model for my children.
- We enjoy traveling together, exploring new places and being outdoors.
- Music is a huge part of our lives (especially rock & country); we really enjoy live music.

The inspirational nature of the intention gives it power (similar to a goal). Since intentions are focused on the quality-of-life situations that are most important to you, it's easy to feel good and excited when you think about your intention. For example, you can anticipate the great conversations ahead, maybe snuggled up on the couch on a winter day or on the back porch with a cool breeze. Being inspired, hopeful, and excited are all emotions that drive positive thoughts and *actions*, so being more motivated will also drive the thoughts, words, and actions that help you achieve your intention. An intention doesn't have the same tangible requirements as a goal (e.g., there's no deadline) or outcome/results focus. It's about being in the relationship, not the outcome of a relationship.

An unmet relationship intention can potentially also make you feel sad, but since much of it relates to how you want to be and show up, you can focus on your part of the equation and your role in the intention. For example, if you want a partner with whom you have sparkling conversations, you can have lots of great conversations with other people while you are on your way to find your partner. As you connect with friends, meet new people and date, you are able to set your expectation for great conversations and savor them when you have them. It's easy to be happy and satisfied when you have a good dialogue with a neighbor, family member, or a new friend. Your focus on good conversations triggers the confirmation bias, which makes you tune in to more good conversations. It's also easier to be positive when the focus is at the conversation level vs. the "will this person make a good marriage partner" goal level. Your appreciation and enjoyment of great conversations helps you "show up" to other people with a positive energy that also helps you achieve the intention.

Specific Characteristics, Interests, Preferences

The third category includes lists of specific characteristics, interests, and preferences (SCIPs) you want your future partner to have. Consider the following examples of categories of these wants and desires you might have for the relationship:

- Personality traits (e.g., extrovert, conscientious, high integrity, ambitious)
- Interests (e.g., photography, sports, outdoors)
- Demographics and background (e.g., Jewish, spiritual, lesbian, Asian)
- Physical features/characteristics (e.g., tall, curvy, red haired, great smile, large bust, etc.)
- Physical fitness preferences (e.g., daily runner, loves hiking, doesn't like physical activity)

- Financial situation (e.g., financially independent, money doesn't matter, no debt)
- Love language preferences (e.g., physical, acts of service)
- Communication style/preferences (e.g., occasional vs. frequent communication, prefers texts to phone, etc.)
- Family (e.g., family of origin, extended family, wants children, has children, empty nester, prior marriages, etc.)
- Tastes (e.g., five-star restaurants vs. casual dining, camping vs. hotels, TV vs. movie theaters, etc.)
- Attitudes (e.g., environmental activist, very private, optimist)
- Political affiliations (e.g., democrat vs. republican, liberal vs. conservative)
- Beliefs (e.g., work ethic, importance of education, right to bear arms)
- Past experiences (where you lived, went to school, sports played, places you worked, etc.)
- Habits (e.g., smoker, exercise fanatic, follows strict routine vs. unstructured days)

Each category on the SCIP list has a couple examples listed in the parentheses to give you a better idea of what might be included. However, you could easily expand each of these categories quite a bit. I could probably list 20+ interests alone (e.g., travel, live music, cooking on Sundays, bike riding, healthy eating, reading, James Bond movies, trying new restaurants, hot air balloon races, outdoor dining, camping, playing the piano, learning Spanish, doing puzzles, etc.). Can you imagine, how many different combinations of characteristics, preferences, and interests are possible between two people?

Many people, at some point, make an exhaustive list of SCIPs. For example, I'm guilty of creating a list of 89 favorite things about my last relationship that I wanted to include in my next relationship. Then there were six additional things I wanted to add to the list. Most likely you also have a few "no's" or deal breakers for things you absolutely don't want in a partner. There are a couple of big challenges with an exhaustive list like this.

First, it's too much. The long-detailed checklist is fatal to the dating process. If you drill down to this level of detail and are interested in finding someone with too many specific characteristics and interests, you could be ruling out a *lot* of people who you might really enjoy being with. The odds of finding all of those options in another person drastically narrows the chance of finding that person as well, right? In addition, after ruling out numerous potential partners who don't meet your checklist, you can begin to believe you are looking for a needle in a haystack. This belief will then be reinforced over and over again as you live out the confirmation bias. If you think this person is too hard to find, they will be.

If you have an exhaustive list of "wants, needs and must haves," you will likely be focused on evaluating each of your dates against the checklist. This "evaluation" can occur whether you are conscious of this process or not. I know this sounds ridiculous, but please remember your busy brain is guiding your conversations and interactions.

Think of it this way. How does a person come across as they are conducting a job interview? Have you been interviewed lately? People being interviewed are often nervous, might filter information to make a good impression, or even lie. This is probably not how you want to start a relationship. Are your potential partners feeling like they are in an interview or enjoying a casual conversation with someone they are interested in learning more about? Who will they find more attractive: an Human Resource (HR) job screener or you?!? What if you were focused on being present and open to learning about your date, free of judgment or evaluation?

Another concern relates to the items on the list. Do you want someone who is just like you or do opposites attract? I used to work in HR and many times managers wanted to hire someone who was just like them, with the same personality and work style. I often wondered if having someone on the team who was exactly the same might eventually drive them crazy? While having some common interests is important, is it a good idea to be a match on too many levels? Doesn't someone who is different make life a little more interesting? Wouldn't it be helpful to have a partner who can complement you on some things?

Another challenge with a long, detailed list of "must haves" and "don't wants" is that we focus on the wrong level of detail. Remember that intention and inspiration happen at a higher conceptual level. Does thinking about someone who is tall, loves camping, and is non-smoker inspire you? These may be features you would like in your ideal partner, but do they inspire you? Remember your emotions drive your actions and being inspired is much more helpful in the dating process than feeling limited and frustrated by having to meet an exhaustive checklist. It's probably more helpful to cast a wider net and at a more attitude or values kind of level.

With a broader, more conceptual list, there are probably a lot of ways these intentions could be filled. For example, caring about health with one person could simply mean you share tips and articles about food and nutrition with each other; with a different person, it might mean cooking together and trying new recipes; for someone else, it might play out as weekly excursions to farmers' markets. Rather than eliminating people who don't align with a specific checklist item (e.g., vegetarian), expand the possibilities of how your intention will come to life in different ways. Meeting new people and seeing how you might learn about the other persons' interests, preferences, and experiences could be a very exciting adventure instead of another disappointing "miss." You might even learn some things and find some new activities you like too. Keep your options open and allow yourself to be surprised and delighted by this process of exploring all the complex differences that make us unique.

Setting Your Goals, Intentions, and SCIPs

It is not difficult to set a goal, intention, or SCIP. One tip is to work from a mindset of inspiration rather than one of sadness and frustration. It seems small, but as you begin paying more attention to your emotions, you'll find that everything seems to go better when you are in a positive frame. You might start by making a list of the things you really liked about your past relationships and partners (the big and the little things) or what you see in other couples you like. Begin to be more aware of what you see around you that you want to incorporate into your future vision. For example, I love seeing couples sitting close together on a park bench. I also get inspired by being with my children and their partners. It feels good to see the way they care for each other.

If you want to create a list of SCIPs, try to keep the list short. Prioritize the most important aspects. Try to focus on the most positive SCIPs. Some people also include a list of things they don't want (e.g., smoker, person who is not emotionally available, drama). This may be helpful in some ways, but not as helpful in other ways. As you can imagine, the negativity bias comes into play here. A better practice would be to look for the opposite. For example, what is the opposite of someone who smokes? Can you add an item about a partner who maintains a healthy lifestyle and takes care of themselves?

One more thing to think about as you are creating goals, intentions, or SCIPs is the availability bias.

 Availability bias: The tendency to think that things that come readily to mind are more representative than is actually the case. When this occurs we tend to overweight that factor in our decisions

If something was wrong or missing in your last relationship, you will likely place a lot of attention on it. Be aware that it might cause you to put too much weight on a single issue because it is dominant in your mind right now. Since it may have been a major contributor to your breakup, it probably is important but recognize where it falls in terms of your priorities and try to keep it in perspective. For example, in your last relationship your ex may have had an issue holding grudges. Therefore, in your next relationship you may want to make sure any prospective partners are able to quickly and easily resolve differences. This may be important based on your last experience, but how prevalent is that issue with the general public? You may not need to put so much weight on it going forward. For example, asking someone how they resolve issues or trying to judge how well they forgive on a first date is probably not a good idea.

Again, keep in mind the challenges related to goals and SCIPs. Setting intentions can be more challenging but have a bigger payoff by keeping you focused on the right level, inspired, and mostly positive. Now that you have direction on where you want to go, it's time to turn attention toward the best way to get there.

Getting It Right

- Your life continues to expand and grow each day with every new experience, and with it, you have an opportunity to identify more and more about what you do and don't want.

- The end of your relationship provided a great opportunity to further clarify your romantic interests and needs. Now you have the chance to define what you want next in a partner and in a relationship.

- This should be a very exciting process. You may be thinking about some big-picture goals for you and the relationship, as well as some specific characteristics, traits, interests and preferences in your new partner.

- There are some good aspects that come from setting relationship goals and thinking about some specific characteristics you want in a new partner, but there are some "watch outs."

- Be careful if you are tempted to make a long list of very specific characteristics, which can substantially narrow the potential pool. In addition, your brain biases could inadvertently make your dates feel more like an inquisition or a job interview, which may cause your date to fail to see what a great person you are. It may also constrain your ability to have a fun date.

- Goals should inspire you rather than cause you to feel pressure to act. The latter may cause you to take action when you are operating from a negative mindset.

- An alternative to setting relationship goals is to set intentions for what you want the relationship to be like. Intentions differ from goals as they inspire you. They focus on quality-of-life issues, how you want to show up and feel when you are together.

- Following the path laid out in this book will help you get what you are looking for in a relationship, and more quickly. One of the first steps is to become more aware of what you want and need, which will also help you find greater happiness.

Chapter Thirteen:

Science of Beliefs

One of the most important things you can do to get the relationship you truly want is to understand the power of your thoughts and your beliefs and how they impact your ability to find and keep the partner you want. So, let's take a closer look at why your beliefs matter and why you will need to pay more attention to your thoughts and beliefs.

While the next section may seem incredible—even unbelievable—try to keep an open mind. There is scientific research backing up these propositions, and many people have reached their goals and objectives leveraging these very principles.

Sometimes a belief can bring about an actual physical result (or consequence). In other words, a belief can cause your external reality to match your internal beliefs. This is known as the self-fulfilling prophecy or the Pygmalion effect.

 Self-fulfilling prophecy: a prediction that causes itself to be true due to the behavior (including the act of predicting it) of the believer.

A powerful, well-researched example of which most people are aware is called the placebo effect. In a typical placebo study, a doctor prescribes a pain pill that is "fake" (e.g., a sugar pill) to a randomly selected group of patients (following surgery, for example), and a true pain pill (e.g., morphine) is given to the other half of the patients. The group receiving the placebo is "tricked" into thinking they are taking a painkiller. Numerous studies have shown that in fact, patients who take the placebo report experiencing the same levels of pain relief as those taking the true pain killer.

The placebo effect is a well-known phenomenon and highlights the importance of the relationship of mind and body. In fact, it is so universally accepted that the FDA requires placebo testing for the approval of new drugs. The tests of the new drug have to show that it impacts patients more than a placebo. In addition, research has also shown the power the *nocebo* effect. In this case, patients who received a placebo (non-active drug) exhibited the side effects of the actual drug even though they didn't get it. This occurred because the doctor's warnings about side effects of the drug created an expectation of the side effects occurring. These expectations were powerful enough to trigger the body's reaction to create the side effects. This provides even stronger evidence of the power of the mind, our thoughts and the mind-body connection.

The placebo effects go beyond pain relief. For instance, in one study, people were given a placebo and told it was a stimulant. After taking the pill, their pulse rate sped up, their blood pressure increased, and their reaction speeds improved. When people were given the same pill and told it was to help them get to sleep, they experienced the opposite effects (Sharma & Sharma, 2015).

How is this possible? Everyone knows that a belief or expectation can't make something physical happen, right? Or can it? One of the most common explanations for the effect is that if a person *expects* a pill to do something, then it's possible that the body's own chemistry can cause effects similar to that of a medication.

Neuroscientist John Levine has done groundbreaking research on placebos and pain. His 1978 study showed that patients don't just imagine less pain with placebos. The pain reduction is triggered by a release of endorphins. The ***expectation of relief*** actually signals the brain to release the brain's natural chemicals that produce the pain relief. The patient's brain becomes flooded with its own supply of painkillers. So the belief that the placebo will help creates a chemical/biological response, a physically measurable impact in the body. A placebo's active ingredient is a person's expectation and the body's response to that expectation.

Many people familiar with the placebo effect may not be too surprised by this information. Returning to where we started in this section, the placebo effect is a scientific example of how our thoughts and beliefs impact our reality. You might be thinking, "Maybe I can buy that this makes sense for our bodies, but surely our thoughts and beliefs can't impact things, people, or situations outside of our bodies." You may be surprised to learn that, yes, your beliefs can also impact both your own and other's behaviors. The following research demonstrates that they can.

Consider a person who spent a lifetime on different diets trying to lose weight. This person might have a long track record of trying new diets, with temporary wins by losing weight but then even larger weight gains followed. Based on these frustrating experiences, their belief in the futility of dieting is very likely to impact their current unhealthy eating and exercise behavior. The attitude and belief that diets don't work in the long run impacts their willingness to eat healthy or stick with a diet or exercise program. This thinking and behavior (or lack of behavior) reinforces the hopelessness of weight loss. This example may seem obvious to you but consider how unaware this person is of how much the belief is impacting their behavior and the lack of results. What might happen if they could change this belief?

Similarly, when we believe something about another person, we may act in ways that encourage them to confirm our assumptions. "When we expect certain behaviors of others, we are likely to act in ways that make the expected behavior more likely to occur." (Rosenthal & Babad, 1985).

Consider the impact of a teacher's expectations on their students. In a study in which teachers were told that a certain group of their students were "going to blossom," those students ended the year with greater improvements than other students in the class (Rosenthal & Jacobson 1968). The interesting part of the study was that the students identified as having a high potential to blossom were randomly selected. They were not picked because of any knowledge, past academic achievement, or ability.

It was the teacher's expectation that influenced their behavior, which impacted the students' progress. Studies have shown that the expectations of teachers have a great impact on learning and development. The positive expectations of the teachers cause them to give more attention to those students, which makes the students feel that they are special and motivates them to work harder and eventually perform well in exams with greater signs of overall improvements. This effect has been replicated in many studies.

We also know from research that when individuals are treated as if they are hardworking and capable, they are more inclined to work hard and believe in their own capability. Conversely, when people are treated as unfriendly or intellectually inferior, they are more likely to act in an unfriendly manner or to doubt their intelligence and keep their deeper thoughts to themselves (Aaronson, 2005).

In the realm of romantic relationships, several studies provide evidence that people's expectations influence, rather than merely reflect, the reality of their relationships (Jussim, 1991; Jussim & Eccles, 1995; McNulty & Swann, 1994). One study demonstrated that rejection expectations can lead people to behave in ways that elicit rejection from others. Rejection sensitivity is the disposition to anxiously expect, readily perceive, and overreact to rejection from significant

> *"If you expect the battle to be insurmountable, you've met the enemy. It's you."*
> ~ *Khang Kijarro Nguyen*

others. The research showed that women who anxiously expected rejection behaved in ways during conflict that elicited a rejecting response from their romantic partners. (Downey, et al., 1998). In another study, researchers found that expectations that a spouse will cheat can contribute to that spouse actually cheating (Biggs, 2009).

Self-fulfilling Prophecy

These studies demonstrate the power of beliefs and expectations on our own behavior and how those expectations impact others' behaviors as well. What we believe and expect about ourselves or someone else makes it more likely to happen.

Most people are not consciously aware of their powerful ability to predict the future. Generally, people don't understand that their beliefs play an important role in bringing about the consequences they expected or feared—it's most often unintentional. However, the impact is the same whether we are consciously or unconsciously aware of the expectation. ***The effect of our thoughts, beliefs, and expectations is not trivial!***

Consider how important these expectations are in getting the relationship you want. Now let's break this phenomenon down in a little more detail to help you see how it works. The self-fulfilling prophecy has four basic parts.

First, it all starts with a set of beliefs. For example, you think, "I really want to be in a relationship and get married, but I've been looking so long and none of the guys I meet ever work out." Operating under the confirmation bias, your brain is focused on scanning for information to confirm your beliefs and expectations. The filter is also ignoring any contrary evidence. So, if you have a belief that there are no "good" men out there, and you'll never meet the right one, you are looking for evidence to support your expectation and ignoring information that disputes it.

Second, these beliefs influence your actions toward others. To continue the example, the woman who wants to meet a man and start a relationship but is feeling hopeless unintentionally sends a message. Let's say she's on a first date. What kind of energy and excitement is she communicating as they meet? What is her body language conveying (e.g., open and interested or cautious and suspicious)? What kinds of judgments does she make about the partner? Considering they don't know each other, if something vague is said, are favorable assumptions made about the meaning of the words? Are these assumptions giving the other person the benefit of the doubt or being used to quickly rule the man out as a bad fit? Remember this may all be happening automatically without conscious awareness.

She may even decide to give him a second chance and start dating him but also have the assumption in the back of her mind that he is probably not "relationship" or "marriage material." This expectation impacts how frequently she communicates, the way she responds to questions, and what she talks about. She will likely not take the relationship too seriously to protect herself from the eventual pain. Or she may cut it off immediately after finding evidence she is "right" based on something he says (maybe even just an arbitrary comment taken out of context). She may be completely unaware of how her thinking impacts her behavior or how her behaviors are coming across. Her intention is to meet someone special, but she has no idea of how she is actually sabotaging her ability to get what she wants.

Third, our actions toward others, shaped by our beliefs about them, impact their beliefs about us. In the example above, the man she meets is likely turned off by her dismissive attitude and behavior toward him and responds accordingly. Sensing her disapproval, he may respond in a guarded way and doesn't invest in the conversation or want to waste his time with someone who isn't interested. Her conversation and responses cause her date to have doubts, and assume she is distant and/or "damaged."

Their beliefs cause them to act in ways consistent with those beliefs toward each other, which reinforces their initial beliefs about each other. Here is where the consistency bias comes into play. All humans want to be and appear consistent between our thoughts, words, and actions, so without even consciously thinking about it, we behave consistently with our expectations. As a result, this woman is not only plagued with looking for evidence the man is a bad match, but she is also compelled to behave as if he is a bad match (e.g., disappointed, aloof, dismissive). The result is that she fulfills her expectation.

He makes a quick exit to avoid wasting any more of his time on something that won't meet his needs. When he leaves, she has more evidence there are no good men. At this point, the woman is convinced he is another man who isn't worthy of her but, at the same time, is simultaneously confused about why she is being rejected. Is it clear how her expectations influenced the outcome? Is it apparent that no man will seem like relationship material when a woman has an expectation and the resulting behavior described above? In essence, it is almost impossible to have a different outcome. Her expectations create reality, which perpetuates the expectations. It's a self-fulfilling prophecy. It's a vicious cycle. You may be thinking, this can't be true. It means you recognize that you may actually be getting in the way of what you want, contributing to your own unhappiness. While this may be extremely hard to hear, if you don't understand it, you can't change it.

Take heart, on a more positive note, we can use the self-fulfilling prophecy to meet someone special and have a great relationship. You do this by changing your beliefs and expectations. Rewriting the example above, having faith in our ability to meet a great partner and have a wonderful relationship can lead to excitement, friendly communication, showing interest, and a great connection on a first date. If the woman begins dating a man she feels strongly connected to, she may feel that this person has relationship potential. Since she expects the relationship to last, she treats her partner with respect and invests more time and energy into making it work.

> *"Whether you think you can or you think you can't, you're right."*
> *~ Henry Ford*

As we've been discussing, this behavior is then reciprocated by the other person and off they go together. This positive attention ensures that her partner is satisfied with the relationship and causes him to invest a similar level of time and energy. Not every relationship will work out, but you can see how the odds of meeting a great partner increase exponentially if you have positive expectations and beliefs about the possibilities.

So far, you now know that in order to get the relationship you want, it's important to set direction (e.g., goal, intention, SCIP), understand the power of your relationship beliefs, and leverage them to get the relationship you want. The next chapter will highlight the importance of a positive, optimistic attitude and being happy. For the purposes of this book, it's not critical to clarify the distinction between being happy, optimistic and positive. You'll see them used interchangeably in the following chapters.

Getting It Right

- Your beliefs are the key to your happiness and success. The scientific evidence of the power of beliefs is so amazing, it is almost unbelievable. However, the research tells the story of how the mind (beliefs) impacts the body (physical reaction).

- Almost as difficult to imagine: your beliefs impact not only your body, but can also impact your behavior and that of others.

- Your expectations create reality! Through the self-fulfilling prophecy, you have the ability to determine your future reality (either good or bad). Your beliefs influence your actions toward others, which impact their beliefs about you, which causes them to act in ways that are consistent with those beliefs.

- If you aren't having the success you want in your dating relationships, look at your beliefs. The best news is that you have the power to change your beliefs and therefore your reality (e.g., find your ideal partner).

- While beliefs are, by definition, ideals you believe to be true, not all beliefs are healthy. Beliefs can change.

- Establish a core set of positive beliefs and expectations about the future you want to create to get the relationship you want.

Science of Beliefs

Chapter Fourteen:

The Importance of Happiness

Think about the people in your life, (e.g., family and friends, colleagues and peers, members of your church, etc.). Can you tell which of them are generally happy and which are not?

We can often get clues about anyone's level of happiness through their words and language. Are they telling stories about fun experiences, happy events, or something new they've learned recently? Or are they complaining about the weather, politics, traffic, or their job? If you want to know if someone is generally happy, pay attention to word choices, topics of conversation, and the opinions and attitudes they express. In addition, you can also get a quick read of a person's happiness level just by watching their nonverbal communication (i.e., the way they carry themselves, the excitement in their voice, or the nervous habits they repeat).

When you are with your happy acquaintances, you can often feel their positive energy; they are likely smiling, laughing heartily, and showing confidence, enthusiasm, and joy. Now contrast the happy person with someone who is unhappy, pessimistic, or predominately frustrated. For example, when you are with unhappy people, you might notice their negative energy through nonverbal cues (e.g., rolling eyes, slouching posture, sighing, frowning, or a more serious facial expression).

Who are the people you want to spend time with: those who are happy or those who are unhappy? There is something very attractive about a person with a happy, positive attitude. People are naturally drawn to happy people. You'll be glad to know research supports this. Optimists are more socially attractive (Böhm et al., 2010). Individuals who display positive, rather than negative emotion, are more interpersonally attractive (Coyne, 1976).

The implications for meeting a great partner are fairly obvious. In a dating situation, first impressions are so important. You will be more attractive when you are happy and have a positive mindset. People will be more likely to approach someone who is happy. We want to come back for more when we spend time with happy, fun, joyful, and high energy people. If it isn't obvious, being happy is an extremely important factor is achieving the relationship you want.

How do others see you? How do you come across to people when they meet you? Do you bring strong positive energy to first dates and consistently along the way in longer-term relationships? The truth is that most people overestimate their level of happiness and optimism. Even if you are a generally happy person, most people can become happier and therefore more attractive. Being happy is extremely important for meeting a great partner. There is a simple test I developed to determine your level of optimism and diagnose opportunities to improve (see Resources).

Being Happier

In some ways does it seem ridiculous to have an entire section devoted to becoming happier? Everyone wants to be happy, right? Being happy feels good, right? Aren't we motivated to be happy? Don't we all try to do our best to be as happy as we can be as often as possible? This seems obvious and logical, but it's not as straightforward as it seems. Somewhere along the way, many people have simply lost their natural sense of joy, happiness, fun, and wonder, and either don't know how to get it back or don't want to.

Are you as happy as you can be? If not, why? Most people of course, will attest to a certain level of *satisfaction* with their lives but would not claim they are extremely happy or joyful most of the time. The General Social Survey has been collecting data on U.S. attitudes since 1972. Below are the happiness ratings for 2018:

"Taken all together, how would you say things are these days – would you say that you are very happy, pretty happy, or not so happy?"

31% - Very Happy
56% - Pretty Happy
13% - Not so Happy

The highest ratings for Very Happy were 38% in 1974. Why aren't we happier? Isn't this surprising when we have such a high standard of living compared to our predecessors?

In the United States, we have a proclaimed right to pursue happiness. The Declaration of Independence recognizes our inalienable rights to "life, liberty, and the pursuit of happiness," yet most of us are not as happy as can be. What gets in the way of our happiness?

For many people, happiness has not been a focus. In fact, many of us may not have really thought about being happy, understand exactly what it is, or how to become happier. Research evidence shows most people don't understand what makes them happy, and *we actually have the happiness formula backward*. For example, you might be surprised to learn that finding a great partner doesn't lead to long-term happiness. It's true that you will likely feel happy in the beginning. The happiness that comes from getting into a relationship is wonderful and electrifying in the beginning. However, the ecstatic happiness typically lasts as long as the "honeymoon phase."

Over time, we and our partners settle into routines, deal with responsibilities, families, and more typical behavior. The passion that comes from falling in love is typically not sustainable and gently drifts into a more stable and regular state. Over time, disappointments, unmet expectations, and frustrations can get in the way of each partner's happiness. For most people, the relationship may be generally satisfying but is not the formula for a high degree of personal happiness alone. Research shows that married people are happier for one to two years after marrying, but after that, their happiness levels are the same as non-married people (Lucas, et al., 2003).

What may surprise you is that *it is actually being happy that will lead you to finding the partner and relationship you want*. In fact, happiness helps us get more of what we want in all areas of our lives.

"Thanks to cutting-edge science, we now know that happiness is the precursor to success, not merely the result… happiness leads to success in nearly every domain of our lives, including marriage, health, friendship, community involvement, creativity, our jobs, careers and businesses" (Achor, 2010).

Much of this research came from the positive psychology movement founded by Martin Seligman. After years of psychological research dedicated to understanding human suffering, depression, and other psychological disorders (aimed at relieving suffering), he decided to instead find out what made people thrive. What he and many other researchers since then have found is that success comes from being positive, optimistic, and happy, not the other way around. It's interesting that his research findings mirror the approach he took to psychology. Stop focusing on the negative and focus on the positive.

People who are happier are more productive in their jobs, are better leaders, and earn more money. They are more resilient in the face of hardship and are more innovative and creative (Lyubomirsky, 2005). Studies have shown that people who are happier are more likely to live longer lives and have healthier bodies (e.g., fewer chronic pain conditions, lower likelihood of diabetes, fewer strokes, higher chance of cancer survival). The estimates are that the happiest people add from five to seven years to their life expectancy (Lyubomirsky, et al., 2005).

In the realm of relationships, happier kids have more friends, are seen as warmer and more intelligent, and less selfish. Having the right balance of positive emotions in marriage makes it more likely that you'll have a greater feeling of love and a sense of fulfillment. In addition, your marriage will be less likely to end in divorce (Simon-Thomas, 2020). Happier people are more sociable and energetic, are better liked by others, and have a better network of friends and social support. *Happier people are more likely to get married and to stay married* (Lyubumorski, 2007).

It is beyond the scope of this book to cite all of the studies, but there is a landslide of research supporting the finding that people who are more positive, happy, and optimistic are healthier, heal faster, and are more successful academically, athletically, and at work (see Resources for studies on optimism). The bottom line is: If you want a good life, including finding a great partner, and have a great relationship, focus on your own happiness first!

Now you might be thinking, "That's all great. I would love to be happier, but my body aches, I have a crappy job and I'm lonely. I can't be happy given my circumstances." This perspective is understandable; however, there may be some flaws in that logic. Researchers have estimated from many past studies that 50 percent of the variance in happiness is based on genetics, 10 percent comes from life circumstances (e.g., rich/poor, attractiveness, health), which leaves 40 percent that is under our control. In addition, as we've described above, being happier can help you *improve* your circumstances. The good news is that almost half of your happiness is based on your thinking and behavior. *You do have the power to become happier.*

So, if you thought that you'd be happier if you had a better job, more money, a hot partner, got married, were thinner, had less physical pain, etc., you've put too much weight on the circumstances. These factors only account for a small portion of your happiness. The following sections describe how happiness works so you can learn to become happier.

How Happiness Works

We know that both beliefs and happiness are critical in getting what you want. Beliefs are a precursor to happiness, and we'll try to untangle your beliefs about happiness. The diagram below shows how they are related and how they influence each other in a cyclical way. Our beliefs impact our thoughts/perceptions, which then impact our emotions, which inspire or discourage our actions or inactions, which impact our experiences (e.g., win or lose), which again... that's right... impact our beliefs, and around we go again.

Your beliefs, experiences, thoughts, and perceptions are at the root of your happiness. If you want to increase your level of happiness, you'll have to understand more about how they operate and potentially change them if they are getting in your way.

Here is a more in-depth look at how the cycle works: Your beliefs come from what you learned from your parents, other authority figures, your religious upbringing, and your own experiences in life. For example, you likely got your work ethic from your family; the belief that you are reliable (or unreliable) from teachers, coaches, bosses; and a belief about honesty or telling the truth from parents or your religion/faith. Your life experiences also contributed to your beliefs (e.g., sometimes it's okay to tell a white lie to spare someone's feelings, I'm great at math, I'm good at making people laugh).

When you experience something (e.g., missed your alarm and overslept), your mind interprets it based on your beliefs and prior experiences. That interpretation is a thought (e.g., this is the second time this month I overslept and I'm going to be late for work) and creates emotions (I'm frustrated, embarrassed, and worried about the repercussions I may face at work). Your thoughts and emotions about this are based on your beliefs (e.g., I have a strong work ethic, oversleeping is bad, I need to make up an excuse about what happened, so I won't be judged or lose my job). Coming full circle, your emotions then stir you to take action (e.g., skipping breakfast so you can make it on time, decision to set a back-up alarm, or facing the music for being late with a mature, apologetic attitude, etc.). This results in an experience that *reinforces* your beliefs, thus completing the cycle.

It is important to understand how this works, so you can make changes that will impact your happiness. Happiness is an emotional state. When you notice an external input (e.g., your alarm goes off in the morning, or you get a phone call from a potential partner), you interpret the input based on your beliefs and thoughts (which are influenced by your prior experiences).

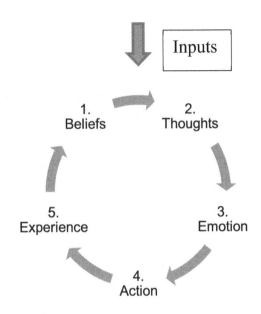

The number and variety of these external stimuli are huge. For example, it includes the people we meet (e.g., friends or rivals), the places we go (e.g., gym, park, or a great restaurant), things and situations we encounter (e.g., cute puppies, beautiful flowers, warm hugs, or a flat tire), or the words we hear (e.g., appreciation or criticism). We also form perceptions about internal stimuli, which could include waking up tired, a nagging thought about a deadline, a memory of a fun weekend, feeling nauseated, or the raised temperature in your face when blushing. As these inputs occur, you form interpretations of the reality you are experiencing. These thoughts/perceptions are often "charged" with emotional reactions (e.g., happiness, joy, fear, sadness), which can give us a positive/happy feeling (e.g., joy or appreciation) or a negative/unhappy feeling (e.g., suffering or frustration).

Thoughts and perceptions can operate without external inputs too. For example, your thoughts anticipating a first date (either positive excitement or negative drudgery) is enough to alter your emotional state during the day as you think about it. For example, on the day of the date you may think, "I feel happy because I have a date tonight with a new person." You may even tell some of your friends you are looking forward to meeting this new person and why you think you like them. Just the state of noticing and anticipating you have a date is enough to make you happy. However, if you have a date tonight and you anticipate it won't go well, your thoughts have created a sense of fear or unhappiness (emotional reactions to your thoughts) that also impact your happiness – or unhappiness in this case – during the day. Clearly your belief about first dates (almost always a waste of time, likelihood of a disaster) impacts thoughts about the date (anticipate fun or misery) which impact your emotions (good or bad mood during the day).

Clearly thoughts, perceptions, and beliefs are important. They have the power to impact your happiness. What if you could change your beliefs and thoughts?

The following story provides some insight into the nature of perceptions and lays the groundwork for the next important principle: changing your thoughts and beliefs.

Once upon a time, six blind men lived in a remote village. One day a villager told them, "There is an elephant in the village today." They had never seen an elephant before and were curious. They decided to investigate.

"Hey, the elephant is a pillar," said the first man who touched his leg.

"Oh, no! It is like a rope," said the second man who touched the tail.

"Oh, no! It is like a thick branch of a tree," said the third man who touched the trunk of the elephant.

"It is like a big hand fan" said the fourth man who touched the ear of the elephant.

"It is like a huge wall," said the fifth man who touched the belly of the elephant.

"It is like a solid pipe," said the sixth man who touched the tusk of the elephant.

They began to argue about the elephant. Each of them insisted that he was right. The truth is they were all correct, right? Based on what they felt, they correctly defined what an elephant was like (based on their unique view or perception of what was available to them).

This story illustrates the point that truth lies in our perspective. Our perspectives are based on our beliefs and experiences, which form our view of reality. Each blind man touched a different part of the elephant and therefore had a different experience and perception, which led him to conclude and believe the reality of what an elephant is differently. *In essence, our perceptions are our reality.*

This is the reason there are always two sides to every story. Each person involved has a different perspective about the information (regardless of how factual the information is) because it is subject to their hearing, understanding, and interpretation. The blind men's understanding of an elephant changed with new information from their other blind friends. Additional perspectives can change our perception, understanding, and therefore the truth.

Here is another example that illustrates how our prior experiences and thoughts change our perceptions of the current state and therefore our happiness. What happens when we get a new pair of shoes? For most women, this experience is fun and exciting. We like everything about it, starting with the way the shoes are attractively displayed, the design or color of the shoes, the experience of trying them on, sending pics to our friends to get a second opinion, the way the shoes are wrapped in tissue paper like a gift when we bring them home, and most of all showing them off for the first time. This is a very pleasant experience for many women.

However, what if you are a woman who has gotten into hot water due to overspending? This woman also enjoys new shoes, but if she maxed out a credit card to buy them after making a promise to her partner to stop buying shoes, she will not likely have the same experience. In this case, that experience of buying new shoes elicits happiness in one person, but in this second example, it is polluted with regret, sadness, and fear. The exact same experience of buying shoes ends in two very different levels of happiness. It all has to do with how we perceive and interpret these inputs.

The key point is that happiness is subjective and is primarily tied to perceptions influenced by prior experiences, beliefs, and thoughts. It is not the shoes nor the new car nor the promotion that makes us happy. It is about how we interpret that thing or event that triggers our happiness emotion. Stay with me here, and I'll bring it home in terms of happiness and relationships. *The best part about this is that if our perceptions become our reality, and we can change our perceptions, then we can change our reality.* We have an opportunity to think differently about how we interpret facts, truth, and what we consider to be reality. If we can alter our perception of our reality, we can change our happiness levels. This may seem conceptual at this point, but the ideas lay the foundation for the sections ahead with more practical ideas to increase your happiness.

Motivation & Beliefs About Happiness

We know that most people are not as happy as they can be. The first points we addressed were that people may not understand the importance of happiness or how it works. We also know that we may have had the formula wrong; happiness doesn't come from getting the things we want, rather being happy helps us get what we want. Beyond that, we also know that many people are *not* motivated to become as happy and positive as they can. This may be due to their beliefs about happiness. Three mistaken beliefs are outlined below.

We aren't supposed to be happy. Some people simply don't believe they were meant to be happy. They may have conflicting beliefs from religious upbringing or family beliefs about the importance of suffering in life. Religious beliefs that emphasize sacrifice and suffering could contribute to your beliefs about how much happiness you deserve. A friend recently asked me, "Isn't life supposed to be hard? Aren't we supposed to suffer?" A related concept is the belief that doing things to make yourself happy is selfish and, therefore, morally wrong. There is also a stigma around being good to yourself and taking care of what you need to be happy. (Part 1, Chapter 6 included a discussion of the importance of self-love vs. being selfish that you might want to revisit.) This is not to say that we shouldn't care for each other, but we need to have balance and ensure self-care is a priority.

Have you somehow adopted the belief that life is supposed to be hard? If so, you wouldn't be alone. Many people have experienced suffering as part of life and have come to expect it as normal. These beliefs may have come from tough experiences growing up, such as challenging family situations, living in a tough neighborhood, poor financial conditions, or failed relationships. We may have adopted this belief based on typical failures we experienced (e.g., school, careers, health, our children, sports, or with friends) without having effective ways to cope.

I can't achieve happiness, so I don't want to try. Others don't pursue a higher level of happiness due to a fear of disappointment. After experiencing a lot of life's challenges, they may have lost hope for being happy. People in this group think that they need money, cars, nice houses, etc. to be happy. Since they see those things as out of their reach, they give up on happiness. Many of these folks call themselves realists. While no life is perfect and we can expect there will be times of struggles and sadness, this does not need to be the predominant state of being.

Satisfied is the best I can hope for. Finally, other people believe that the most they can hope for is to be satisfied and content. They may believe that their lower level of happiness is predetermined as their fate. Some understand that we are destined to experience a full range of emotions and know that happiness is just one emotion. They do not expect to be able to be happy all the time and do not realize they have the power to increase the balance or predominance of happiness in their lives. Just because we won't be happy all the time doesn't mean we shouldn't pursue happiness. While there is a lot to be said for being satisfied, there's so much more available in life. Don't settle for contentment when true happiness and joy is within your reach.

Can Beliefs Change?

So now the challenge is knowing or learning how to make yourself happy. This journey toward owning and creating your happiness needs to start *before* you find your partner. Remember that we have the happiness formula flipped around? Happiness comes first, before we get the things we desire. Being happier also makes you more attractive to potential partners.

Since happiness builds on our beliefs, we need to start there. By definition, a belief is something you think is true. While the majority of the beliefs you adopted were good and helpful, some may not have been as beneficial. As we've discussed, many of our beliefs were handed down to us when we were young by well-intentioned parents, teachers, or religious representatives.

We also added to our personal library of beliefs based on our experiences. For example, if you were the last kid picked to be on the soccer team in grade school, you might have drawn the conclusion that you weren't good at soccer... or worse, that people don't like you. As young children who didn't have all the tools to properly evaluate our experiences, we may have drawn inaccurate conclusions about our experiences.

Then the negativity and confirmation biases kick in and that negative experience happens again reinforcing your belief. Now you form a self-fulfilling prophecy which locks in this downward spiral unless something interrupts it. Obviously as an adult, you can see that the child might have needed some skill coaching or confidence building before writing off themselves off as a bad soccer player—or worse assuming that people don't like them! Your imperfect ability as a child to process the information may have resulted in a belief that was wrong and doesn't serve you.

Whether our beliefs came from others or we formed them from our own experience, we accept them as truths. However, as a result, most of us end up as adults with a cadre of limiting beliefs based on our trusting acceptance of information from others or our imperfect, immature interpretations of our experiences. When a belief puts limits on our potential, damages our self-esteem, or our relationships, we call it a limiting belief. Because of the self-fulfilling prophecy, these beliefs, perceptions, and experiences become reality.

Here are some examples of some of the beliefs I had that did not serve me well:

Old Belief	New Belief
I have to be perfect	*I am okay with my imperfections (most of the time).*
Always put others first	*Put my own oxygen mask on first before I can help others.*

Doing things for other people is being nice	*In most cases, it is harmful to do things for other people when they are capable of doing them for themselves, especially if there's a chance they may begin to believe they can't do it for themselves.*
I'm not good enough	*I am good enough and deserve all the good things life has to offer. I have the power to create the life I want.*
If I follow all the rules, I'll be happy	*Following all the "rules" makes other people happy. I need to set my own rules and boundaries for what makes me happy.*
Never go to bed angry or I have to resolve conflicts as quickly as possible	*It's okay to wait until my emotions settle before resolving a conflict. It is better to sleep on it, so I can gain perspective the next day. It's okay to have negative feelings and I don't have to resolve them immediately.*
Moms have to be superwomen	*Trying to be all things for all people is a formula for disaster.*

In the past, we may not have considered objectively whether our beliefs are accurate or true. More importantly, we need to consider if these beliefs are good for us.

What is even more challenging is the fact that we may not even be consciously aware of these limiting beliefs that operate in the background of our minds guiding our thinking, decisions, words, and actions. The limiting beliefs show up as the voices in our heads. We all have them, whether we are aware of them or not. Most of us think of this chatterbox in our minds as our own voice, but actually it comprises the voices of the people in your life who have influenced you, the beliefs you adopted as a naïve child and accumulated as adults.

While we obediently pay attention to what it says and follow through with action, it is often not in our best interest to do so. It is very important to be open to the idea that our beliefs may not all be truths and to understand how we can challenge the limiting beliefs that get in the way of our happiness. Some family beliefs (e.g., work ethic) and religious beliefs (e.g., golden rule, sacrifice) may take on an even stronger element of truth and may therefore be considered sacred cows (infallible truths that cannot be questioned). Even these sacred cows might need to be challenged.

Have you ever had a belief about something and then later learned it was wrong? Sometimes it happens when we have a person on a pedestal and then they fall from grace. This often happens very publicly with politicians or celebrities. Or we might hear another side of a story and change our mind about an issue. A common example many can relate to is your belief in Santa Claus and the Easter Bunny. Your parents very innocently planted this belief in your young mind, with the good intention of making you happy during the holidays. As a child, you held onto this belief and, even after you may have had your suspicions, continued to hold onto the belief until you were confronted with the truth. While this is a simple example, it makes the point that you had a belief that was given to you by your parents and society, you thought it was truth, and it guided your thoughts, decisions, and actions (e.g., be good so you get presents). Then you learned it was not true and changed your belief. So, if it was possible with this belief, could some of your other beliefs be incorrect also?

Remember the story of the six blind men and the elephant? Each of them had a different experience of the elephant independently and their own, but different, beliefs about what an elephant was. They were each correct based on their own unique experience. However, each of their beliefs was incorrect too. With additional information and perspectives, they were able to change their beliefs.

Considering that many of our beliefs came from other people or childhood experiences, isn't it logical that we take a look at them as rational adults and see if we want to continue to be influenced by the beliefs that may be causing problems? Are there some beliefs that we don't want or need anymore? An important step in becoming happier is a willingness to examine and challenge our beliefs... particularly the ones that do not help us.

Having an open mind and a willingness to challenge the validity of our beliefs is a big step. It doesn't necessarily mean that you'll change your beliefs, certainly not all of your beliefs, but being open to examining the ones that are not helping you is important. If you can look at your beliefs, understand more about where they came from, if there are other valuable perspectives to consider, and most importantly whether having that belief is helpful or harmful, you will have a better chance of happiness in your life. You may decide that some of your beliefs aren't serving you and may need to be eliminated or replaced. Going through the process as a rational adult can also help you recommit to the beliefs you choose to keep.

Next, let's turn our focus to beliefs about happiness. What are your beliefs about happiness? The pursuit of happiness is actually very elusive to many. You may find that you have a belief that you aren't meant to be happy, suffering is virtue, your happiness is ruined forever (due to a divorce or some other significant loss), or that there isn't anything you can do to improve your life and be happier.

I had some limiting beliefs about happiness too; however, I spent some time thinking about my happiness beliefs and I also did some experiments to alter my state of happiness. These experiments consisted almost exclusively on changing my beliefs and thoughts. A good example would be my beliefs about how I worked. Many have described me as a workaholic, and in the work culture, that wasn't an insult. In some ways I was proud of what I had accomplished, and it felt good to succeed. I had a very high standard for what needed to be done, at what quality level and by when. I was not willing to fail, but there was a price to pay for sure.

I really believed I didn't have a choice. I believed this was what was expected of me, but I also learned that part of it was what I expected of myself. For example, I began experimenting with showing up for a meeting without being completely prepared by having a full-blown recommendation in hand for an important meeting. Instead, I engaged the group in developing the recommendation together. Guess what? I won. I got out of the office at a decent hour the night before, no one was angry I wasn't prepared, and the group got engaged in the solution.

These types of experiments showed me that I could replace some of my limiting beliefs and be happier with different beliefs. Based on these experiments, my more recent experience and choices, I now have the following beliefs about happiness:

- *We were all meant to be very happy.*
- *We can become happier.*
- *I can choose my thoughts, and my positive thoughts make me happier for substantial periods of time in my life.*
- *I like being happy and enjoy feeling good!*
- *Positive emotions and happiness snowball; the more often I'm happy, the more I experience happiness in my life.*
- *I am enthusiastic about life, and this energy is noticed and felt by other people. It is attractive. People like my positive energy and enjoy being around me (for the most part).*
- *I will not be happy all the time, but when life gives me lemons:*
  - *I know I will be okay, and everything always works out in the end.*
  - *I know if I acknowledge and process my negative emotions, they will not grab a long-term foothold over my life.*
  - *I know tough times will pass, so the bad times are not as awful.*

- *I know I have an opportunity to reframe and think differently about any problem or loss.*
- *It gives me an opportunity to appreciate the times in my life when things are going great.*

Let this sink in for a minute. Read through the list again. You deserve to be extremely happy and you can be. Do you believe this? Are you living like you believe this? Don't forget that being happy is a reward in and of itself, but it is also an important element needed to help you find a great partner and have a satisfying relationship. Let's look at how you increase your level of happiness.

Getting It Right

- When you think of the people you enjoy spending time with, would you describe them optimistic, enthusiastic, and happy? Now contrast that with people you know who are negative and pessimistic. When you are with your happy people, you can often feel their positive energy. They are likely smiling, laughing heartily, enjoying life. Happiness is attractive!

- Research shows that people who are happier are more productive, are better leaders, and earn more money. They are more resilient, innovative, and creative. They are also more likely to live longer lives, have healthier bodies, and a longer life expectancy.

- In terms of relationships, research also show that happier kids have more friends. Happier adults are more sociable and energetic, are better liked by others, and have a better network of friends and social support. ***Happier people are more likely to get married and to stay married.***

- Many people believe they will be happy when they find their partner. Research shows that we have the happiness formula backward. Being happy will lead you to finding the right partner, not the other way around.

- Your happiness is in your control. It comes from your perceptions and is highly influenced by your beliefs and thoughts. In order to change your happiness, you will need to examine your own beliefs to determine if they are true for you today and if they are serving you. It's important to eliminate those that don't.

Chapter Fifteen:

Increasing Happiness

What makes you happy? While what makes each of us happy is very unique, there are some generalities we can make about what makes most people happy. It generally falls into three categories: things, experiences, and memories. When researchers ask people "What makes you happy?" they might give examples like getting a new car, presents, having enough money to pay the bills this month, a bigger house, a promotion at work, etc.

This category is described as ***Things/Situations***, and they are the most popular responses to the question, "What makes you happy?" While we believe that things will make us happy, that happiness doesn't seem to last very long. When was the last time you got something tangible that really made you happy? How long did that feeling last? How long did it take before you started thinking about the ***next*** thing you wanted? ***Research shows that happiness that comes from attaining things is very fleeting.*** The academic name for this is Hedonic adaptation; the happiness that comes from getting a new phone, car or job will wane over time.

 Hedonic adaptation is the tendency for humans to quickly adjust back to their normal level of happiness after a happiness boost that comes after getting something.

Money is a special exception here. People believe that more money will make them happier, presumably so they can buy the things that they want. Research shows your emotional well-being rises with your income, but only to a certain extent. Once a person reaches $75,000, there's no greater happiness associated with higher income (Kahneman & Deaton, 2010).

Experiences describe the next category. Examples might include watching your child play soccer, a great first date, running, Sunday brunch with friends, walking barefoot in the grass, going on vacation, getting married, etc. There is a lot of happiness associated with experiences and you get the added benefits of anticipating the experience and then extending the fun by looking back with fond memories... (part of the next category). *The big "take away" here is that experiences make people happier (Boven & Gilovich, 2003), and they have a longer lasting effect on happiness than things (Kumar et al., 2014).*

The last category includes *Thoughts, Reflections, and Imagination* and is a much less popular response. In this category, people might mention remembering how great it used to be to play carefree as a child or looking back over photos of a recent ski trip. It can also mean thinking, visualizing, or daydreaming about the future. For example, spending time thinking about how great it will be to lose 10 lbs., imagining what it will be like to find our next partner, or visualizing the expansion of your small business. Another great example in this category includes spending time in meditation or in gratitude for what is happening or has happened in our lives. For now, keep in mind *this category is very powerful, completely available to you at any time, there is no cost, and very few repercussions from indulging in these activities.* We'll return to this category in the next chapter with some ideas to leveraging these mental processes to get the relationship you want.

Do the Things That Make You Happy.

Take charge of doing the things that make you happy. Sadly, many people have forgotten what makes them happy. If this is the case, you'll need to do some work discovering or rediscovering what makes you happy. This list of ideas is endless based on people's unique interests. If you don't really know what you want, you could start by referring back to Part 1, Chapter 6 for ideas on doing things that might make you happier after your breakup. Next, think about what you enjoyed as a child or anything that made you smile or brought you joy in the last month. Be willing to try old things again or some new things or activities.

If there are things that make you happy, but you believe they will only make you happy if they come from a partner, don't wait. Buy yourself flowers, jewelry, and make nice meals for yourself. Go to concerts, on bike rides, and to museums, etc. It's great to bring a friend if one is available, but don't let not having a companion stop you from doing what you want to do. This is a great opportunity to enjoy your own company.

This is all part of the journey toward learning how to make yourself happy. Although you may have a belief that you can't go to a movie theater alone, or it's not as much fun to go by yourself, do it anyway. Test that assumption. Is it really less enjoyable or were you simply concerned with what these total strangers sitting around you would think about you being alone? Will you ever see those people again? Does it matter what they think? Get past those fears. Learn to completely enjoy your own company.

Having an open attitude about meeting interesting people in general is a winning formula. When I'm alone, I'm much more likely to strike up a conversation with a stranger, and I find other people are more willing to approach me as well. You never know what is going to happen or what connections you can make. You might meet a lovely couple and they might end up being great friends, you could find a professional connection you need, the tennis partner you were looking for, or you might get introduced to a friend of theirs who could become your next love interest. Be open to possibilities. Of course, that's not the reason you talk with them, but once you start opening the door to enjoying meeting people and *being happy by yourself*, watch for all kinds of great surprises.

One of the most important points is to make your happiness a priority sooner rather than later. Too often we put ourselves and our own happiness last, and years can go by before we notice we have formed a habit of surviving or just barely being satisfied. Give some thought to how much of your day, week, month, or year is devoted to doing the things that make you happy. For many of us, we are caught in a world of obligation and responsibility and spend only a small percentage of time doing things that make us happy. It is often our lowest priority. There just isn't enough time.

There are two approaches to changing this pattern. First, we can dedicate more time to doing things that make us happy. You may have to make some trade-offs to find time to do the things you like and have fun. Of course, there are things we all have to do (e.g., feed our children, go to work, etc.). The alternative leads to consequences that would ruin our happiness today and in the future. However, you may be able to give up some "should do's," "want to do's," and even some "need to do's" that could be reconsidered to see if they are absolutely essential (e.g., cleaning as often, making meals from scratch, attending the church gathering). Some activities such as watching television, surfing the web, etc. are generally considered less value-added when it comes to happiness. While finding more time for fun is a great step in the right direction, it likely won't be enough to raise your happiness to your desired levels.

For most of us, raising our happiness substantially will need to come from more than just squeezing in more rewarding or pampering activities. The second approach is to weave happiness into everything you do. Incorporate fun, positive thoughts, and a good attitude into your regular responsibilities every day. You can be happier even when you are doing things you "have to do" or may not like to do.

> "And what matters about positive emotions is not making them last or clinging to them but having mild positive emotions frequently. That seems to be the strongest predictor of satisfaction with life, with positive trajectories of growth, and so on" Fredrickson (2015).

For example, can we make work activities more interesting or be happier while we are engaged in them? Instead of the drudgery of laundry, why not make Tuesday night a family laundry-folding party? Everyone meets around a bed or a table and tackles the pile of laundry together. Tell jokes, have a contest to see who can fold the fastest or fold the most perfect towel. The times goes faster when everyone is together laughing and talking, and the work gets done much more quickly with a lot of hands. Have some time in the car on your commute? Use travel time to connect with people (safely) on the phone. If you don't enjoy cleaning the bathroom, turn up the music and sing and dance your way through the work. Look for more ways to incorporate more happiness into your life.

We spend a lot of hours at our jobs. This is another place you might be able make more enjoyable by changing your mindset. Take a minute or two before a meeting starts to ask about someone's weekend or tell about yours, laugh at yourself if you make a mistake, go into an intense meeting with a mindset that everyone can win. If someone gets under your skin, remind yourself about something you like about that person before tackling a conflict you need to address. These small mindset shifts can make amazing improvements in your experience. Give it a try.

Play is often an overlooked source of happiness for adults. Give some thought to the things you used to play as a child. Can you start playing adult soccer, join your kids in the backyard in a game of kickball, or play a card game with your friends? Ask the kids in your life or watch the children in your neighborhood to help you brainstorm ideas—they are experts at fun!

Reframing: Change Your Mindset

Since happiness is the result of our thoughts, perceptions, and how we interpret situations and events, we should also be able to change our unhappiness when bad things happen—without any change in our circumstances. We can do it all from within, by changing the thoughts we assign to what happens.

There's a helpful tool to reduce unhappiness with your everyday life activities called framing. It's based on how you view or think about the events or situations in your life. Your interpretation or the meaning you assign reflects the picture "frame" you put around them. The color, material, size, and shape of the frame around the picture can enhance or detract from the beauty of the picture. The same is true of how we think about the events in our lives. We can react to a situation (the picture) by framing it positively or negatively.

Here is an example related to dating to make the idea of framing clearer. Let's say you have dated someone three times and things seem to be going well. You really like them, but before your fourth date, they call and say, "I'm sorry but after getting to know you better, I've realized we just don't have a long-term connection." How does your brain interpret this?

Person A: "I can't believe this happened again. Women keep breaking up with me after a few dates. What am I doing wrong? I'm so tired of being rejected, I'm just going to quit dating for a while. I wish so badly I could meet someone special. I'm tired of being alone."

Person B: "Well, I'm a little surprised by that call and disappointed, but I am grateful she called me instead of stringing me along or ghosting like some other women have done. It's good that we won't waste a lot of time together if she's not feeling it. I enjoyed our time together and her company, but there's nothing lost. I'm also very grateful I didn't go into a downward spiral feeling rejected by this call. I've come a long way. I'm sure it's just a matter of time before I meet someone who's a good match for me. I enjoy meeting new people and am looking forward to the next opportunity. Life is good!"

So, the facts are the same, but the interpretation and attitude are very different. Person A is setting himself up for the self-fulfilling prophecy, the negativity and confirmation biases to reinforce a very negative memory trace, and future negative experiences. Person B is able to put the breakup in perspective and not take it personally. He looks for the silver lining and is therefore happier and more likely to attract a partner than person A.

The different perspectives described above are good examples of framing. The picture (breakup call) doesn't change, but our experience of it changes based on the frame. The frame can enhance the picture by drawing attention to beautiful colors or detract from it by clashing or distracting from it.

The concept that reality is based on perception allows us to actually change our reality. If we choose to focus on more positive aspects of our situation, we change our experience of it. Then when we are focused on the positive things, our brain is programmed to seek out more positive things and de-emphasize the negative. ***Through this process, we can in fact change our reality***. It may seem like a radical thought, but as discussed, many of our beliefs were not developed rationally and do not serve us today. Changing your negative thoughts and beliefs is definitely worth exploring.

Now you might be saying, "Sorry, I don't buy it." Maybe you've tried to be more positive, but it doesn't seem to work. When beliefs related to situations are big, have been around for a while, and are particularly painful, they will likely require more work to eliminate the negative thinking before the power of positive thinking can take root. For example, if you believe "My marriage is over, my heart is broken, there's no sugar coating this – no reframing is going to make this better." In these cases, you'll have to process the trapped negative emotions before the positive attitude can take root. Go back to Chapter 11 to process trapped emotions. You may also want to start on something that is not terribly big or painful. To get started, consider some experiments on a smaller scale. Are there less painful situations in your life where you can try the power of positive thinking and get some smaller wins?

I understand. I tried positive thinking and failed. Many years later after connecting the dots on teachings from experts in this area and my own experimentation, I learned what had been getting in my way. I found I had to quiet the negative voice in my head before the positive thinking could take hold. I personally experienced the power of reframing my thoughts (and processing negative emotions), and then became a more positive, happier person. However, even with this knowledge, the pain of my breakup made it very difficult to shift to a more positive frame, but eventually it did, and I know it speeded my healing and recovery.

Get Over Stuff Fast

We all have trials and tribulations throughout the day. These occurrences can disrupt our happiness. How do you maintain your happiness when bad stuff happens (e.g., argue with your partner, kids are fighting, your hair starts to turn gray or fall out, or you have problems at work)?

Remember your goal is to tip the scales, so you are creating a lot more positivity to minimize the impact of the negativity bias. So, roll with the punches more, let small offenses roll off your back, make a decision to let things go. Worry, regret, fear, guilt are not our friends and aren't worth wasting energy on. There is no good that comes from them. Remember, we can change our feelings by changing the perceptions; reality is overrated. Forget about your mistakes, remember your successes.

I remember early in my career getting advice from a mentor to never take offense when something happens. At the time, I didn't understand what she meant. I was appropriately upset. I had just poured my heart into a project and it was cancelled. I took the news as a personal attack. I thought I was powerless over being offended—it just automatically happened.

*What I couldn't understand then, but now know, is that we can chose how we see and react to information. Today I know that if someone is upset about something I did or said, it's almost always more about their issue than mine. I can listen respectfully to what they have to say and give them what they are asking for (if it fits for me), but I **decide** for myself how I want to interpret and respond (be offended or not). A helpful mantra for me is "What they think about me is none of my business." It's taken a lot of practice but building this capability has been incredibly helpful in getting over things fast.*

I've also had great luck with trying to keep a big-picture perspective about things that go wrong. For example, I've had enough life experience to tell me that by tomorrow, next week or next month, I won't even be able to remember the troubles of the day. Even the big important ones don't make a big difference over time. If I can remind myself that time is a great healer, and I know I'm going to be okay soon, why not just let it go today? Feeling bad today, or the next week or month doesn't help anyone, and it takes a toll on me.

One additional practice that has been helpful for me is to remember the self-fulfilling prophecy and the power of my thoughts. When something bad happens, I now use the opportunity to ask what else might be going on below the surface. I take a look to see if there are any subtle, unconscious thoughts that might be surfacing problems through the confirmation bias or the self-fulfilling prophecy. Since I know that my thoughts have power to make things happen, I also know I can change my life if I change my thoughts. I don't need to worry about reality because I know I can change my life. Therefore, it's easier to let problems go faster.

Change Your Beliefs that Don't Work

If you notice you seem to have a pattern of feeling worry, regret, fear or guilt for example, it may be helpful to do some pre-emptive work to make it easier to deal with these emotions more quickly when they come up.

One of my emotions that seemed to be a problem pretty regularly was guilt. Tackling my beliefs around feeling obligated and guilt helped me get over the situations that made me feel guilty more quickly. I grew up in a religion and family that leveraged guilt to convince members to do what we were asked to do. I learned it well. As an adult, I eventually decided that doing things I didn't want to do out of fear and obligation wasn't a winning formula and was often hijacking my happiness. I also recognized my own ability to apply guilt and manipulate my children to do what I wanted them to do.

I didn't figure this out until they were teens, and it may have been a little late, but I made a decision to stop. I declared that we were going to be a "no guilt family" and said it often. Sometimes they reminded me too! It made a big difference in all of our lives. As I did a better job saying no to obligations, I learned to let go of my feelings of guilt and fear of making people angry when others pushed back. This ability to let go and move on happened more and more quickly when I hit challenges.

The best part is that because I try not to make anything an obligation (except for weddings and funerals) my kids want to spend time with me. Based on what I see with other families I feel extremely grateful about this. One last note: we are never too old to change. I was able to make the shift and so were my teenagers who are now adults passing on the "no guilt family" to their children.

If you get triggered by something negative and have a hard time "letting it go" or feel yourself starting into a downward spiral, refer back to Chapter 11 (Diffusing Negative Emotions) to process your negative thoughts and feelings. You can get over stuff faster if you take a few minutes to FYF when it happens.

There's another practice that can be helpful to change your beliefs: the use of afformations, a term coined by Noah St. John (2014). Have you ever noticed that when you are trying to remember something but then give up, many times the answer will eventually come to you, often later that day? This is because your brain keeps working on it.

Afformations leverage the power of this continual search process to reinforce a belief. It involves reciting a positive affirmation but with the twist of stating it as a question. For example, your afformation might be: "I wonder why it's so easy for me to meet amazing men and have fabulous dates?" The confirmation bias kicks into gear to find reasons to support your afformation. Stating it as a question propels the brain to not only confirm but seeks to answer the question to close the loop.

To bring this example full circle, when you state the afformation about finding amazing men and going on fabulous dates, your brain is scanning your environment all day to prove that you are right! It filters out information that doesn't support the statement. These cues of support, reinforce the truth of your belief, raise your confidence and positive emotion, which changes your attitude, behavior and creates a self-fulfilling prophecy. Better dates and partners are on the way.

Gratitude

Being grateful is an incredibly powerful tool and attitude changer. There is much written about how to establish a gratitude practice and the impact of making that simple mind shift. It also aligns very well with framing.

You could easily start by identifying three unique things you are grateful for each morning and then again at the of each day. Soon you'll find yourself grateful for more throughout the day (remember the confirmation bias). It can definitely snowball and be a positivity multiplier. It takes no money or extra time; it can simply become a practice of how we look at the world differently. You can use gratitude to reframe most negative or neutral situations. Look for the silver lining, remember you can learn from everything, and whatever is going on can look different and better tomorrow.

Belief in Something Bigger: God/Higher Power/Universe

It may be helpful for you to align with your religious or spiritual beliefs when you want to become happier. If you have spiritual beliefs, what do they say about your purpose in life? Is God's[1] plan for you to be happy? You may be surprised to know there are well over 100 references to joy in the Old Testament and 60+ in the New Testament (depending on which Bible version you read; see Resources).

If you are looking for a new or different way to frame your religious or spiritual beliefs, consider that God resides inside each of us. So, your unique dreams, goals, and desires were actually planted there by your god/creator. God is in your corner, rooting for you, supporting you, and wants to help lay the groundwork to achieve your dreams. God is your collaborator, and your biggest cheerleader, not your

---

[1] For brevity, God will be interchangeable with universe/higher power, etc.

punishing judge. Try to visualize or think about how your God sees you, with love, kindness, and hope.

Research shows that many people find happiness in giving back and service to others. This can be formal in terms of serving on a committee, foster parenting, volunteering at an organization you believe in and contributing financially, or it can be informal like reaching out to a sick friend or talking with a lonely neighbor (Otake et al., 2006).

Meditation and Mindfulness

Our busy brains may not cooperate to easily help you quiet negative thinking about not having the relationship you want and might need some help allowing more positive thinking. One tool that can be especially helpful in quieting our busy brains is mediation. Many people have found significant shifts in their levels of peace, happiness and positivity through the practice of mediation. There are many types of meditation (e.g., open awareness, guided, progressive/body scan, sitting, mantras, mindfulness). Mindfulness techniques provide tools to help individuals become more aware of and less judgmental of thoughts and ruminations (Teasdale et al., 2000). The popularity of these practices has grown substantially, resulting in a large variety of resources and support available online, in your communities, and even through popular phone apps. A couple of these websites are listed in the Resources section.

Visualization/Imagination

Have you ever thought about the power of a movie to make you feel incredibly happy or sad? Why is that? Nothing changed in your life. Your experience thinking about the scenes in the movie were enough to alter your mood. If this can happen through a movie, can't you create a change in your happiness by thinking better thoughts?

Our brains can't tell the difference between experiences as they are occurring, remembered, or imagined for the future. Therefore, the impact and benefits of happiness can be created without being in a real situation that makes you happy. Your own imagination is a very powerful way to create happiness.

You can enhance your happiness by 1) anticipating with eagerness things and experiences you are looking forward to, and then 2) savoring or remembering the things that happened in the past (even earlier in the day can be helpful). For example, are you having breakfast with a friend, playing tennis this afternoon, having a first date with someone you have been chatting with online, or going on vacation next month? These are things we can look forward to with anticipation. During and after breakfast, tennis, the date, or vacation can you recall the memories and savor the moments? You can do this the next morning, later in the week, or anytime.

There are several ways this approach can help you. First, think back on the happiness you can remember from any and all relationships from the past. For example, did you enjoy sharing the details of your day together, exercising together, singing your favorite songs, or sitting on the back deck in the evenings? Do you remember the places you went together that made you happy (even if it was the hardware or the grocery store)? These happy experiences can be helpful to think about with all of your past partners and with other relationships (including family or friends).

Remembering these good times can help you recreate your happiness. The next chapter includes suggestions for using your imagination to create your future relationship. Keep in mind we can conjure up happiness in any situation with very little time and no money through our thoughts alone. It's fairly simple. Just spend time imagining the things you'll do with your new mate, the places you'll go, the experiences you'll share together. The better you feel when you engage in this exercise, the more likely you will be to create what you want.

Music

Music has the ability to alter your mood. After a relationship ends, a sad country breakup song can bring most of us to tears. In a similar way, there are songs that make you feel so good you might burst out singing or maybe even dance. It's actually pretty amazing how quickly it can shift a mood. Studies have shown that music affects many important aspects of life and health such as memory, mood, cardiovascular function and athletic performance (Harvard Health Publishing, 2011).

Putting together a great playlist and listening to it often can help you shift from a negative to positive mindset. This is not a substitute for processing emotions, but it is a happiness boost that can be very effective as a complement to FYF for many people.

I actually have several different happy playlists. For example, one with slower songs that help me feel grateful and peaceful (e.g., Sara Evan's "I Could Not Ask for More" and Natalie Merchant's "Kind and Generous"); another is for bubbly happy songs (e.g., Pharrell William's "Happy,"

Maclemore's "Glorious,"). I found that even the process of creating playlists was a good distraction and listening to music became very therapeutic for recovering from the breakup, and then shifting to a happier frame of mind.

Getting It Right

- As it turns out, there are many things you can do to increase your happiness, and none of them require money! In fact, research shows that the happiness that comes from getting "things" is less than anticipated and is very fleeting! Experiences give us much great happiness.
- You have the power to increase (or decrease) your level of happiness by your thoughts without changing your circumstances.
- If we choose to reframe our experiences by focusing on the more positive aspects of the situation, we change our perception of the experience of it which then changes our reality.
- Since beliefs impact your perceptions, reconsidering your beliefs and potentially changing the ones that limit your happiness can have a profound impact.
- Discover or rediscover what makes you happy and then take charge of doing those things.
- Being happy alone often opens doors and leads to great surprises, so make your own happiness a priority and don't be afraid to do things by yourself.
- Practicing gratitude, a belief in something greater than you, leveraging your imagination, listening to music, and meditation practices can all impact happiness

Chapter Sixteen:

Putting the Positive Relationship Mindset into Action

So far, this ongoing section has laid a conceptual foundation and rationale for why you need to adopt a positive relationship mindset. Now let's leverage this information and provide more practical tips for dating and finding the relationship you want. Some of the information may have been mentioned previously in different parts of the book, but here we have a chance to pull it all together with some practical advice to get on the right track.

If you do one thing: ***Remember the most important thing you can do to get the relationship you want is to pay attention to your thinking.*** You probably don't need to change the dating site you are on, your profile, or your appearance. Your work is to examine your beliefs, how you're thinking, and figure out what's in the way. The self-fulfilling prophecy is very powerful! Accordingly, Part 3 started with a challenge to set expectations (e.g., intentions, goals) for what you want. However, it's not enough just to set an expectation. You must pay attention to the thoughts you think, the words you say, and the messages you send that align with those thoughts. Here are a couple of examples about why this is so important.

I know someone who hates the dating process and feels like the options for good partners are very limited. He saw dating only as a means to an end; something he had to endure in order to get to a long-term relationship. He described dating as going to a junk yard, sifting through the carnage, looking for the least damaged person. While it was an entertaining description, I am not at all surprised that he had a miserable dating experience. As we know, the confirmation bias causes us to scan for information that supports our beliefs and filter out any information that doesn't support our beliefs. His negative thinking set his powerful radar to look very intently for the dates who have "damaging baggage" and emotionally healthy people likely didn't even show up on his radar screen—therefore proving him right over and over again. This is very easy to do, especially when we are operating under the influence of powerful biases to quickly evaluate people.

Another person I know often referred to her "10 years of being alone" after her divorce in conversation. She was convinced she would never find anyone to remarry, and I'm quite sure that on her current path, she is right. She also talked with anger and jealousy about other women who found someone else in a relatively short amount of time. After all, she had been alone for 10 years since the divorce. It was incredibly unfair.

It was difficult to hear her talk repeatedly about how no one understood what she's been through and how impossible it was. Understanding the power of our thoughts and words, I cringed every time she threw out the phrase "these last 10 years being alone" (which she said often). Her hopeless, angry thinking, and words had a lot of power. Perhaps she tried to be more positive at different times, but she lost hope after so many years. I am very empathetic to her experience. It's hard to ignore the reality of what was happening. I understand and am sad for her experience and long-term pain. I also know that as long as she continues to talk and think in those terms, it cannot change for her.

The most difficult idea here is that *we have power over what happens in our lives*. Occasionally, I tried to argue with her a little and share concepts like the self-fulfilling prophecy, but she only fought me harder saying I didn't understand. Maybe she needed to hold on to her hopelessness. Maybe she needed to feel like a victim. Maybe she needed to be right. I could understand that. The idea that we are responsible for creating the miserable situation we are trapped in may be more than some people can handle. I only know that she won't get what she so desperately wants until she can change how she thinks and talks about the past.

It might be obvious to see the damage this negative way of thinking and talking has in others, but it's much harder to see this happening in ourselves. Many people are not consciously aware of all the beliefs, words, and thoughts that occupy their minds, much less how thoughts impact their results. This chapter will provide some practical ideas and considerations around dating, online dating, sex, and visualization about your next relationship. I'll then also share ideas that may help if you are still stuck and not getting the relationship you want.

Dating

If thinking of dating as a trip to the junk yard is not a good mindset, what is a winning mindset? Let's start at the beginning, with an example of a first date. Before you go, start by setting an intention to have a good experience; expect to be delighted. Try not to think of it as a means to an end. For example, if you are thinking "I have to go on these dates to sift through 20, 30, or even 100 people to find someone I want to be in a relationship with (and who wants to be with me)", dating may feel like a job or a chore. Alternatively, the attitude that will accelerate the process of finding a partner for a relationship is to *enjoy the journey*. Instead of thinking of dating as work, think of it as kicking off your next great adventure. Think of it as part of the story you'll look back on fondly with your new partner. At a minimum, plan to enjoy making new acquaintances.

Try not to put too much pressure on the date; simply go to enjoy another person's company. Relish the idea of learning about someone new. With the right mindset, you can keep the first meeting light and have some fun. Most importantly, set an intention to like the person. It doesn't mean you have to marry them, but *why not be predisposed to like the people you meet?*

Once you are on the date, try looking for the best in the person. Ask questions, listen, and be interested in learning about them. Try making a mental note of the things you like about the person. There should be at least one thing you can find to like about every person. If you can't, maybe that's something for you to work on. If it's comfortable, let them know what you like about them as a part of your conversation. For example, "You have a good sense of humor," "I like your accent," or "that was a great story." Hold up a mirror (so to speak), so they can see what makes them attractive and special. Offering a genuine compliment can feel good for you and your date. Looking for good in people and minimizing what you notice that's bad can reinforce your happiness too. Try it. You are more likely to sustain your good mood and have fun on the date.

If you notice something you don't like, try not to pay too much attention to it, at least not early on the date. Here are some tips for getting past that. 1) Look for clues that your initial negative impression might be wrong (remember the negativity and confirmation biases), especially if your concern is a deal breaker. This is one of the ways to overcome confirmation bias. Since your brain is looking for evidence to reinforce your perception of something bad, you can make a game of looking for evidence that it's wrong. 2) Ask questions to check your assumptions. Give your date the benefit of the doubt until you can confirm the information or impression. 3) If you find out that you are in fact correct, try to minimize the attention on the negative information and focus instead on the things that you like about the person and their strengths. If the date doesn't go well, it will at least make your time more pleasant.

I know a woman who is a professional dater. She wants very much to be in a long-term relationship and has never given up on dating, but she's been at it for decades. She had so much experience and became highly skilled at finding problems, warning signs, and deal breakers right away. I believe she was proud of her ability to "diagnose" her dates and rule people out fast. She never asked my advice, but if she had, I would have suggested she experiment with shifting her focus from faults to strengths. For every one thing she didn't like, find ten things she did like. I also wonder about the impact of biases on her quick evaluations with her finely tuned list of "watch outs" and "warning signs." I truly hope she finds the relationship she always wanted, but I suspect that her approach may be getting in the way.

You should also balance your interest in them with sharing something about yourself. Talk about your interests, the things you like to do, and let them know what's important to you. This mindset can make a difference in your experience with first dates. You'll start to have more good first dates and will likely have more second and third good dates too.

After meeting your date, if you know they aren't a fit, let them know as early as possible, with as much honesty and respect as possible. While it is hard to seemingly reject someone, it is kinder to be honest. In most cases, they will understand the "rejection" is not personal because they are in the same dating game. They probably don't feel a connection with everyone they meet either. Of course, it can be more difficult when the other person wants to continue the relationship and you don't, but follow the same formula regardless.

Let them know that you just aren't feeling the connection or the chemistry (even though there were many things you liked about them). If possible, let them know a few things you specifically liked about them. Skip this if you can only give somewhat general compliments (e.g., you are attractive or a really nice person); they come across as insincere flattery. If you like the person, you can offer to continue seeing them as a friend, but don't do this if you don't mean it.

I've heard through the grapevine that being friends after dating can never work, but I've got some great friends who started as dates. On occasion, I have been pressed by dates to tell them what they did wrong or what I didn't like after we broke up. I don't believe this is helpful because

*people are all so different. Just because it was something I
didn't like, it doesn't mean someone else wouldn't. However,
if the person was sincere about learning, and there were
things I thought might help with other people, I have shared
the information in the most respectful way I knew.*

Online Dating

How do these ideas apply to online dating? One of
the biggest challenges with online dating is that we are
forced to make our initial choice of a date based on a photo
(that may or may not be what the potential partners really
look like). Yes, some sites provide additional profile or
personality information, which can definitely be helpful.
However, consider the massive complexity about people we
looked at earlier in the book (e.g., SCIPs—background,
family situation, interests, hobbies, preferences, etc.).
Capturing this complexity in a profile is nearly impossible.
We all know that it is hard to figure out what to say, how
much to say, or how to sum up who you are in just a few
words. The accuracy of the information may seem
questionable, and the people with good marketing skills are
probably getting better dates.

Remember that it is your mindset that is most
important here. The question is: How do you feel as you are
swiping through people? If you feel good and excited about
the possibilities, then you are in a great place, but if you
struggle with the process, the next section offers some
suggestions to make it better.

There are a couple of reasons you might like online
dating. First, there is an extensive menu of people to choose
from. You recognize you are not alone when you realize how

many people like you are looking for a love connection. It's pretty easy to date. You communicate with a person who might be a match, decide to take it to the next level, and meet. It can be an efficient way to find the kind of person you are looking for. It feels safe, especially if it is challenging for you to introduce yourself or meet people in the general public (e.g., bar, event, or other social gathering).

There are also reasons you might not enjoy online dating. You may have had bad experiences such as people misrepresenting themselves. You may believe you won't find anyone online (since you haven't yet), or you've had bad luck with potential partners responding to you. It may seem like a waste of time or may not feel right to disregard someone with a swipe. If any of these scenarios resonate with you, here are few ideas to make it easier.

Before you begin an online session, set an intention about how you want to think about the people you'll view. For example, you might ask for inspiration to guide you as you consider potential mates. You could set an intention to have an open heart, a focus on love, caring, and respect. You could wish each person you view peace, health, and/or happiness. If you are a spiritual person, consider offering a blessing or prayer for each person as you swipe past or show interest. While this may seem like a useless or unnecessary thing to do, *remember the power of your thinking.* When you send an intention to be your best self and think the best of others, you will be in the right frame of mind to find the best mate.

Sex and Dating

Sex and dating is such an interesting topic because there are so many different beliefs and interpretations of what having sex means in the context of dating. It is a great example of the mind-body connection. It can simply be a purely physical delight, an expression of love and appreciation for another person, a way to create and bring new life into the world, and maybe 20 other things in between.

Despite all the complexity, sex is a wonderful way to feel good. It's more than just the spectacular elation or fulfillment that comes from climaxing, although that could be enough reward in and of itself. Sex satisfies a basic human physiological need for touch (Maslow's Hierarchy of Needs, Chapter 1), provides a lot of pleasure, and can even be healing. The Resources section in the back of the book includes a link to the Touch Research Institute at Miami University with a listing of more than 100 studies demonstrating the healing power of touch. Research shows for example regular physical contact with premature babies increased weight gain by 47 percent, students were twice as likely to speak out in class when teachers patted them on the back in a friendly way, and massage therapy reduced pain in pregnant women and alleviated prenatal depression (Keltner, 2020).

It's one of the few ways we can simultaneously meet our needs as well as the needs of another person (e.g., Physical Touch—Language of Love, Chapter 6). In addition, there are benefits from connecting with another human in a very intimate way. Through the intimacy of sex, we can experience a profound sense of being loved.

These are enormous benefits to be sure. However, there are also some big challenges. The focus here won't be on the physical risks (e.g., unwanted pregnancy or STDs), but rather the emotional and self-esteem challenges and opportunities.

One of the most important questions you encounter with dating and relationships is whether or not to have sex and when, or how soon in the relationship. Just like everything else we've talked about in the book so far, the key to answering these questions is to understand how you *feel* about it, what your beliefs about sex are, and why. You likely have a lot of different and maybe even conflicting beliefs about sex. What are your beliefs, where did they come from, and are they serving you today? It may also be helpful to think about your purpose for dating. Your purpose likely impacts your actions and beliefs. For example, if you are dating to find the love of your life and get married, your beliefs around reputation and exclusivity may be in the forefront (especially if you haven't been married before). If you are dating after a recent divorce to get out there again to explore, you may be more interested in recreational sex.

Here are some examples of typical beliefs people might have. As you scan the list, see if you identify with any of these beliefs. If so, it's important to determine if the belief is serving you, and if not, what action you can take to change your belief.

Recreation/Physical Need

- Sex is awesome, and I want to have as much as I possibly can.
- As humans we have a physical need for sex.

Love

- Having sex is the ultimate expression of love.
- Sex is best with passion and romance.

Reputation:

- If I have a lot of sex partners, I risk ruining my reputation, which limits my opportunities for a long-term relationship with some partners.
- There is a certain number of sex partners that are okay before I ruin my reputation.
- There is a number of dates (e.g., 5) you need to go on before having sex will spoil your reputation with that partner.

Obligation:

- After we've been dating for a while, I owe it to my partner to have sex.
- My date spent a lot of money on our night out, therefore I should have sex.

Convey Interest:

- I need to have sex to communicate my interest.
- If I have sex, my date will overestimate my level of interest.
- If my date doesn't have sex with me, they are not interested in me.

Exclusivity:

- Sex should be reserved for a long-term relationship.
- Sex should be reserved for exclusive relationships.

Limited Pool of Quality Partners:

- There are a limited number of partners available who will be interested in me.

- There is a limited number of partners I am interested in.

Types of Sex:

- Some forms of sex are more acceptable than others.
- Some forms of sexual activity are not considered "sex" in terms of ruining a reputation.

Body Image:

- I am afraid if my date sees me naked, they will lose interest (and vice versa—I will lose interest) .
- I am not physically attractive, and therefore need to have sex to attract a partner.
- I only want to have sex with physically attractive people.

Performance

- I need to be an excellent lover to attract and maintain a partner.
- Having sex is very important to me. We are both adults. I can't help if my date gets hurt.

You may have some of these beliefs or have very different beliefs. As we've reviewed throughout the book, many people have beliefs they aren't aware of. Some of these beliefs may be sabotaging you. In addition to your own beliefs, when it comes to sex, you may layer on beliefs about what *you think your ideal partner may or may not want.* This makes sex in the dating game very complicated. It's important to be clear if your sexual activity is driven from "fear or fire (passion)."

For example, you may want to get married, and believe your ideal partner will only be interested in a spouse with a "good reputation" (few sexual partners). So you are likely to limit the number of partners you have sex with to people you believe are excellent prospects for the long-term relationship. However, this can be a dilemma because you take a gamble on whether the person you are dating should be one of the few.

There's so much pressure to know if this relationship will last. You may want to wait so you can make a better determination about your prospects with this person. However, you might also be concerned that the person you are dating will misinterpret your reluctance to have sex as a lack of interest in them or sex. Thus, you are plagued with a conflict (a problem either way). If you have sex and the relationship doesn't last, you not only have to contend with the loss of the relationship, but now you've "wasted" one of your "sex partner placeholder slots" (the number of sexual partners you believe is acceptable [e.g., 3, 10, 20] before you get a bad reputation). If you make a bad bet too often, you could cross the threshold of what is considered acceptable, so you fear you'll never find a great partner. Now you are also beating yourself up for mistakes that cannot be fixed. While this is an unfortunate scenario, it can change if you are willing to rethink your belief system.

There is also an important interplay between sex and self-esteem for most people. Many times, beliefs around sex can damage self-esteem. Several examples are provided below. Keep in mind, true self-esteem comes from inside, it's an understanding of your own value and worth without regard for what you do or how you look (Self-Esteem, Chapters 1 and Self-Love Chapter 6).

There is enormous pressure to "perform" well during sex. Being a good lover and knowing how to please a partner may be a source of personal pride. This is awesome (especially for one's partner) unless, their sense of self-esteem is tied up in this ideal image. For example, this person may be putting too much weight on what they can *do* that makes them attractive to a partner, instead of *who they are* (which is aligned with their authentic self-esteem). For those with a conquest mindset, having sex with a lot of partners may seem to raise their self-esteem; however, this is an artificial boost because it is not focused on their value as humans. In addition, because this approach may not sit well with all of their sexual partners, it could backfire if those partners attack their self-esteem by complaining of feeling used or deceived.

A person who is not performing as well as they would like could lose their confidence and may even decide to stop having sex to avoid embarrassment or attacks to their self-esteem. This is a big challenge with dating because potential partners may assume the individual is "not into them" or not interested in sex and may move on. Similarly, people who have gained a few extra pounds and have body image issues, may decide sex is too big of a risk to expose themselves to potential ridicule. They may actually fear their own harsh self-criticism as much as they do another person's, so they similarly avoid engaging in sexual activity to protect their self-esteem. On the other hand, if someone who is struggling with body image, and nevertheless becomes vulnerable and has sex, this may enhance their self-esteem because they make a decision to value themselves as a human as opposed to a magazine model.

Hopefully, the examples provided point out some of the potential landmines associated with sex and dating. Most of the beliefs listed above would likely lead to being self-critical and/or damaged self-esteem, which could limit you from getting the relationship you want. It's also likely that performance fears and body image issues impact your performance as well as your enjoyment of sex. It's unfortunate because there are so many big benefits to having a healthy sex life. However, based on what we see in our society and maybe in our own lives, the beliefs and conflicts can cause problems (i.e., negativity and confirmation biases again).

The question for you today is what your beliefs about sex are and whether they are serving you? If not, do you want to change them? Can you untangle the unhealthy beliefs to have a more fulfilling sex life? Return to Chapter 15 to review some of the best practices for changing your beliefs. In addition, if you are carrying regrets, beating yourself up for past mistakes, being angry at people who have lied to you or used you, it may be time to forgive yourself and possibly them (see Forgiveness in Chapter 6). If you think you may have hurt other people, you may decide to apologize to them. It is not necessary but may help you move forward free from any potential negativity weighing you down.

Before closing this section, there are two last ideas that might help you. First, your beliefs related to what you need to do, not do, or be in order to be attractive to your ideal partner may be particularly destructive. Ironically, they may be getting in the way of getting the relationship you want.

There are multiple challenges here. These beliefs are based on what you *think those ideal potential partners believe*. Can you know what someone else believes without asking them? Can you really assume that all of your ideal partners think the same? Do you want to base your behavior and decisions on someone else's beliefs? Don't fall prey to the scarcity principle and the fear that there are only a few great matches for you. This may pressure you to conform to others' desires. It's much more important to identify and focus on your own needs, values, and beliefs.

Second, if you are interested in another way to think about sex and dating, maybe this philosophy could work for you. Advance the progression of your relationship, on both the mind and body levels, in parallel speeds or timeframes. In other words, match the progress of your physical intimacy with the pace of your mental/emotional intimacy.

For example, when you date someone, you likely take your time getting to know them. On a first date, you might share where you work, talk about our hobbies, the music you like, etc. You probably keep the sharing pretty light, which is appropriate in the beginning. After more dates, you might talk more about your family, political beliefs, past relationships, where and how you live. As the trust builds over time, you might open up and share some of your more vulnerable personal perspectives (e.g., your shortcomings, sexual preferences, and your dreams for the future). A healthy rule of thumb is to mirror your physical intimacy at a similar pace as your emotional intimacy. The progression on the physical side could include holding hands, a first kiss, touching their face, stroking hair, putting your arm around them, snuggling up while watching a movie, being physically present as a couple meeting friends/family, public displays of affection, and of course ultimately having sex.

If you are in a place where you trust someone with your body before you can trust them with your personal thoughts and emotions, things may be out of kilter and it's much easier to get hurt. Another benefit to waiting is that when you have sex, there's some trust, so it's easier to have open communication and guide your partner toward what you like and vice versa. There's a good chance the sex will be better, which gives you a better chance of a longer relationship. Contrast that with having sex that is not satisfying too early, and it ends the relationship. This might have been avoided if the couple had waited until there was more trust and open communication down the road. If your date is not interested in thinking the same way, that would be a good sign that there may not be a good fit. What is the rush? If you are in it for a long-term relationship, why not invest in a few more dates?

To wrap up the section on sex and dating, if you are looking for the answer to the question we started this section with—whether and when to have sex, the answer lies in your beliefs. The answer is inside of you. Make your decisions about sex based on your own beliefs (without concern for what you think your partner will think of you). Next, figure out if any of your beliefs need to be replaced so you can live worry, conflict- and regret-free (at least when it comes to sex).

Imagine and Visualize

The last chapter described the process of visualization and how it can help you be happier. This section describes a couple specific ways you can put your imagination into action to get the relationship you want. This may not work for everyone, but some people find success with daydreaming or visualizing their new relationship; it can help accelerate making it happen.

You can create a vision for the future. Go back to your goals, intentions, and/or SCIPs. Visualize how you'll live, where you'll live, how you'll spend your time, and how you will feel being together. Think about the vacations you'll go on together, your wedding (if this is something important to you), the great sex you'll have, or how you'll grow old together. This is a great place to weave in the best qualities and aspects of past relationships with the additional things you want to create in your next relationship.

Dream a little, make believe, and pretend. The more vivid the visualization, the more powerful. Use all of your senses to help make this more vivid and real. If you can include sights, smells, sounds, and feelings, the more likely it will create the emotionally charged memory trace that brings you joy.

Here's another suggestion for how to take this to the next level and have some fun with it. Play a game with a trusted friend where you tell them all about your fictitious, imagined new partner (but tell it as if it is real). Share the details about how you met, what you like about them, what you enjoy together, where you go, etc. Yes, I'm talking about pretending. Maybe you can play this game with a friend who is also looking for a partner and you can both swap stories. After you have your first conversation you can follow-up with texts about how great it is going, where you went together last night, what they said, or how happy you feel.

Keep the story alive. Each time you do this, you'll be giving yourself another happiness boost, which will bring you closer to getting what you want.

I heard of someone who took this positive thinking as far as cleaning out a section of her closet to make room for her new partner. Now that is confidence about the future! The main idea here is to feel good talking about the new relationship. If it helps to tell the story, or clean out a drawer, go for it. Feeling positive and hopeful will help you achieve your goal.

You probably won't be surprised by the warning label on this practice. If you've been paying attention, you'll know that you don't want to do this if it makes you feel bad. If visualizing makes you think, "I'll never find them" or "I wish I had them now" or if any part of the daydream makes you feel bad, stop. To combat this, flood your thinking with positive thought and emotion. It may also be helpful to go back and process the negative emotions before you try this exercise. However, if this technique works by getting you excited and feeling hopeful about your future partner, leverage it.

Obstacles: Still Not Getting What You Want?

If you find you are not getting the relationship you want, examine what you are thinking, your beliefs, and the kinds of message you might be subtly sending. It's a mind game. There are four possible causes we'll explore: 1) overpowered by subtle negative beliefs, 2) myths about relationship happiness 3) myths about partners, and 4) personal beliefs.

#1: Overpowered by Subtle Negative Beliefs

The first and one of the biggest problems to dig into is the idea that your biased mind could be playing tricks on you. There's a good chance that you might be *so* focused on getting into a romantic relationship that the strongest thought active in your mind is *actually* the negative thought that you *don't* have the relationship you want *now*. This thought, even if very subtle or unconscious, may be overpowering your hopeful thoughts and therefore sabotaging your ability to meet someone great.

An example of a subtle negative belief that may be keeping you from finding your ideal partner is based on the scarcity principle, another bias.

 The scarcity principle, says that things are more attractive when they are in high demand and short supply.

If you have a belief that there are very few great partners for you, then they will indeed be very hard to find (remember the confirmation bias). There are a couple reasons you might think this. You might believe you have one true soulmate, which implies almost impossible odds of finding that person. Or you might have been dating for some time and based on your experiences with a lot of dates, might have concluded that your ideal partner is extremely difficult to find—a needle in a haystack so to speak.

If you have the belief that finding your ideal partner is very difficult there's another complicating factor that makes getting into a great relationship even more difficult. The other limiting factor is the idea that out of the small number of potential partners *you* might like, *they* must also like you. Now the pool of potential matches got smaller again. Since you believe there are so few good matches, you may also believe you have to do everything possible to make a relationship work if you are lucky enough to find someone. This may add unnecessary pressure to then conform to what you think they are looking for in a mate. Changing yourself to meet someone else's ideal is not a formula for your happiness or for the success of the relationship. When the relationship inevitably doesn't work out, you now have more evidence that it's almost impossible to find your ideal partner, thus fulfilling your expectation.

If you have these types of beliefs, you may want to reconsider. What if you change your belief about the availability of ideal partners? Remember the scarcity principle is another bias, sort of a mental trick. Is that belief serving you in some way, or is it possible that the belief is an obstacle? Where did you get the idea that there is one true soulmate? Have you loved more than one person in your life – why only one? Is it possible that the idea of one true partner was sold to us by the movie industry? This romanticized fantasy is likely doing much more harm than good. Is it possible that you are clinging to it as a rationale for being alone? Is the belief that there are few partners for you accurate? Have you done the research on the population statistics where you live?

If you expect there are few ideal partners, then that is what you experience (your brain searches for evidence to confirm this and filters out information to the contrary). What if you adopt the belief that there are so many acceptable partners to choose from, that you need to be very picky because there are so many options? This would likely minimize your concern about their desires and could focus more on your own. Although if this is hard too hard for you to believe, maybe start with the expectation that you will easily find at least one good partner. This would create a different self-fulfilling prophecy and be a healthier perspective that could eliminate self-sabotaging thoughts and behaviors.

Another great way to accelerate your success and break out of the thinking about the lack of a relationship is to stop thinking about a relationship (or lack of one), and instead think more broadly about connecting with people in all kinds of relationships (not just romantic ones). This may be especially important if you have a long and/or painful track record of bad dating or relationship experiences that are strong blocks to thinking more positively. The negativity bias is powerful and so is the reality of your experience.

Having fun and enjoying other relationships that are less emotionally and negatively charged can help turn the tide toward more positivity for a romantic relationship. I realize that this may seem like a detour postponing you from finding a partner now, but your urgency and possible desperation may be what is getting in your way. Keep in mind that Chapter 7 (Helpful People) is dedicated to connecting with people. Appreciating and enjoying your existing relationships, the excitement of making a new friend, and being friendly with strangers puts you in a frame of getting what you want faster.

Here are some specific ideas:

- Can you shift attention toward spending more time with your existing friends, family members, professional colleagues, or neighbors you enjoy?
- Is it time to be adding new friends?
- Can you set an intention to have a pleasant interaction with each stranger you encounter (e.g., smile at the people you pass on the street, strike up a conversation with the person in the elevator with you or line behind you at the grocery store)? You can even silently offer a kind thought to each person you encounter in your day, without them even being aware you are sending it.
- You can set your radar to watch for examples of love everywhere around you and take a moment to appreciate them.

Turning on your radar to watch for the signs of people caring for each other, paying attention to the best features of good relationships from all of the people around you can change your energy. What you focus on expands, so you'll be priming the confirmation bias to look for more evidence of good relationships. After trying some of these practices, you'll be surprised by how this can create an attitude shift in you. As a bonus, remember that the positive energy you give off also makes you even more attractive

As I've mentioned earlier one of my favorite experiences is seeing a couple holding hands. It gives me such a warm feeling. There's something comforting about

this little, gentle, public demonstration of caring and love. Holding hands with my grandson (e.g., even when we are simply crossing the street) can give me the same thrill. Obviously, it's not the same, but the feeling I get from holding his hand is close to the feeling I get from holding hands with a partner. Observing examples of love between other people or getting those feelings through other experiences makes me happy.

#2 Myths about Relationship Happiness

Let's turn attention toward some common relationship beliefs that may be getting in your way. Why do we dream about being in a relationship and having a great partner? Because we believe it will lead to our ultimate happiness. This seems like a reasonable expectation, but let's unpack it a bit.

To start, remember that research shows that we have the happiness formula backward. Instead of thinking you'll be happy **when** you find the perfect relationship, you need to be happy to find a relationship you want. But what about your happiness in the relationship? Will being in the relationship make you happier?

If you've been in a relationship before, has this been your experience? Were you happier in the relationship? If yes, for how long? Is this what you've seen in others' relationships? Are the majority of people you know who are in relationships very happy or would you describe them as satisfied and content? Remember that research shows people were happier the first two years after getting married, but afterward had the same level of happiness as non-married people (Lucas et al., 2003). This is not to say that it's not worth it, but let's be clear about the relationship's ability to sustain your long-term happiness—it won't.

However, there is a lot of research showing that people who are happy, positive, and optimistic have better relationships. More specifically, optimists demonstrate higher levels of satisfaction with intimate relationships and have longer lasting friendships (Geers, et al., 1998). Optimism leads to more satisfying and longer lasting relationships (Srivastava et al., 2006). Finally, optimism is associated with better relationship quality, fewer negative interactions, and with higher levels of cooperative problem solving (Assad et al., 2007).

If you are generally not happy without a relationship, does it seem realistic to think the relationship can make you happy? I would argue that happiness doesn't come from a relationship; it comes from inside of ourselves. ***Become happier, attract a great partner, start a relationship, and then continue to rely primarily on yourself for happiness.***

*My grandmother's husband suffered a nervous breakdown when she was a young mother with two children in high school. He was institutionalized and spent the rest of his life in hospitals and long-term care facilities. Tragically, she lived the rest of her life as a quasi-single woman. She had a husband, but the marriage was a legal status only. After the children grew up and moved away, she lived alone as a single woman. I'm extremely empathetic about her predicament. She was married to a man who couldn't be a husband, but in those days, she must not have felt she had the choice to divorce and be in a loving relationship. Growing up, I remember noticing that **every** time we visited,* *she asked about whether I had a boyfriend, was in love, or she tried to fix me up with someone she met.*

While I mostly brushed her questions off, as a teen, I started to understand they sent a powerful message to me. The message I picked up was that my life wasn't okay if I wasn't in a relationship. I mistakenly thought that since I understood what was happening intellectually, it would not negatively impact me, but I was wrong. Awareness wasn't enough to keep my young brain from being "brainwashed." The idea that I needed a partner to be happy infiltrated my psyche and drove many decisions in my life (even when I was rationally aware it wasn't true). The belief that I needed to be in a relationship to be ok and be happy was not serving me (remember the happiness formula). I needed to process the emotions related to that belief and replace it in order to get out of its clutches.

There are so many different beliefs we each have about partners and relationships. You'll need to discover your own helpful and harmful beliefs. You may want to give some thought to the words and phrases you use repeatedly. If you aren't aware of the phrases you use when talking about relationships, ask a friend to help you. Another option is to ask yourself how you are feeling after you talk about dating or finding a mate. If you feel energized and excited, you are likely having healthy thoughts. If, on the other hand, you have painful, frustrating emotions, they are pointing toward negative thinking and beliefs.

If you don't like how you are feeling about relationships, you'll need to change your thoughts. Is there anything positive you can say? Find the littlest things you can find to say or think that are hopeful and positive, as long as they are authentic. Start with the small things because they are easier to believe, and then you'll have some wins and can build momentum. For example, you might think, "The last time I used an online dating site, there were several people I was interested in. There's no reason to think I won't find a few more if I look again this time." Or "I have new information about dating from this book that I think will really make a difference in my dating luck!"

Keep your relationship intention in mind with every text message, first date, and encounter you have with potential partners. Of course, they all won't be exactly what you want, but if you begin to adopt a philosophy of expecting the best and being open to recognizing the value of everyone you meet, you will begin to notice a shift in your experience. More of your first dates will be good, more of your potential partners will show interest, more of the high-quality partners you want will show up. The results may start small, but they can quickly multiply.

#3: Myths About a Great Partner

A common assumption in relationships is that our partners can make us happy by what they say, or do, or don't do. For example, someone might say I will be happy when my partner shares the household responsibilities equally, remembers our anniversary, buys me great gifts, gives me space when I need to be alone, and talks to me about what is bothering them before the problem grows out of hand. Isn't it reasonable to expect my partner to make me happy?

Well, when you consider all of our unique and complex preferences, needs and desires, not to mention how they can change over time, making another person happy is an extremely tall order. It can lead to joy when they get it right but can also lead to frustration when they get it wrong. Even if a person understands what makes their partner happy, their interest and ability to deliver it consistently is questionable. This task is incredibly challenging, even for the most eager and capable partners.

What happens when our partners don't deliver? If they can make us happy, then don't they also have the power to make us unhappy? Since all humans have limitations in terms of their understanding, willingness, and ability to deliver on our needs, putting our happiness in someone else's hands seems to be a dangerous proposition that can set us up for disappointments. In essence, by expecting our partners to make us happy, we are handing over the control for our own happiness to someone else. So, what is the alternative?

A better solution is to take full responsibility for my own happiness in the relationship. Then my partner doesn't have responsibility to make me happy but can *enhance* my happiness. This approach ensures that I own, steer, and control my own happiness and make sure I get it right. When the responsibility lies with me, I can manage my level of happiness. It also takes the pressure off of my partner. This actually helps them be a better partner because they are focused on their own happiness. A happy partner is more attractive which helps keep the relationship alive over time.

Relying on this philosophy means whatever additional happiness my partner brings to me is just the icing on the cake. If I am responsible for my baseline happiness level, my partner can enhance my happiness but cannot reduce it, even if they disappoint or frustrate me. Of course, there are some extreme circumstances in which our partners can profoundly impact our happiness (e.g., cheating, breaking up, physical or emotional abuse, illness, death). However, in terms of everyday living, our partners can't take our happiness away. This may be a new and challenging way to think about relationships, but it can be very powerful and can help you get the relationship you want and keep it.

When two people enter into a relationship, each taking ownership for their own happiness and self-care, magic happens. The couple is full of appreciation and excitement for each other. This is what real chemistry looks like. When difficulties arise, they know how to manage their own emotions and detach from their partner's issues in a healthy way without getting triggered. If they encounter conflicts, they are able to communicate clearly and easily from a balanced place of both caring for themselves and their partner. This is the ultimate relationship; it is a living demonstration of unconditional acceptance, appreciation, and love.

#4: Personal Beliefs

The final set of beliefs that may be sabotaging your ability to get in a relationship you want are your beliefs about yourself. You might be unnecessarily critical of yourself, may not be taking care of your emotions or your needs. You may be aware of ways you are self-critical and hard on yourself... or you may not. If you aren't aware, ***one of the signs that you are overly harsh on yourself is if you are critical and tough on other people***. In other words, you may hold others to a very high standard because you are holding yourself to a very high level of accountability too.

Why are we so hard on ourselves? First, it's important to recognize that all people have value and some people do not understand their value. Perhaps as children they received messages from well-intentioned but imperfect adults who told them that they didn't measure up. Maybe they were criticized harshly for mistakes and didn't know how to make sense of the negative words hurled at them. For many of us, the adults who guided us didn't know how to help us understand the best ways to deal with criticism, negative thoughts and feelings. Beyond childhood, some people may have had trouble coping effectively with tough challenges or failures as teens and adults. Maybe they decided they weren't as good as other people based on their comparison with others at work, in social settings, in magazines, or on television.

To understand more about whether this is happening for you, listen to the voice in your head. If the voice is primarily encouraging, supportive, and positive, you are in good shape. If the voice is casting doubts, critical of you or others, then shut it down. Remember, that voice isn't you. The voice came from well-intentioned, people in your life (or from your own bad experiences). The voice reflects the flawed reasoning of a naïve child who did the best they could to navigate life. You don't have to listen to it. Change the radio station so to speak.

I have a vivid memory of myself as a child running away from a situation crying, "I hate myself; I hate myself." Why would a child say such a thing? I honestly don't remember what happened that upset me, but I have the sense that I upset someone and was angry at myself for whatever I did. Something in my life didn't add up and my young mind turned the confusion into anger at myself. I didn't know how to process the idea that I am a good person regardless of my mistakes or that my value didn't change whether people were angry with me or not. I believe that I carried these flawed ideas forward in my life. That simple immature processing drove me to avoid anger and question my value for much of my life. What's worse is that I wasn't aware of this, it was not conscious.

So, what is the cost of these experiences and beliefs? In terms of my fear of anger, I have walked on eggshells being careful not to upset people to avoid their anger. This focus on making and keeping other people happy in relationships often meant that I didn't take care of my own needs and interests. I lived the golden rule putting other people first... but not in a healthy way. I'm also aware that I suffered the pain of perfectionism, making choices because I needed to feel successful in order to be okay.

I also recognize that what I learned wasn't all bad. My drive for perfection likely helped me finish a Ph.D. while raising three kids. My fear of anger helped me communicate and work effectively with all kinds of people and situations. But understanding these issues today helps me know that I can cope and handle it if people are angry with me and if I make mistakes. I no longer have to avoid anger or put others' needs before mine. My value doesn't come from what I do any longer. It comes just from being me. These insights and the subsequent healing came through the work of processing my emotions and beliefs. It was only through uncovering these faulty messages that I've been able to combat these ideas and minimize their negative impact on me as an adult.

Being hard on ourselves by not taking care of our feelings is a form of self-abandonment. When we are emotionally healthy, we recognize and acknowledge our feelings (all of them, even the tough ones), learn about what they are telling us, and do things that are in our best interest. *If on the other hand, you avoid emotions, don't process them, or do things that are not in your best interest, you will likely attract and be attracted to partners who have similar self-abandonment patterns.* They don't know how to love themselves or you. If you are in a relationship with someone like this, you might secretly hope they will see what you do for them or acknowledge your caring nature and return your love. The problem is that they don't and probably can't.

One other kind of person you may attract if you lack self-care is a person who manipulates others into taking care of them and their feelings. This person may seem to be interested in you, but is actually only doing this to influence you to take care of them. This person doesn't know how to care for their own feelings. They need other people to placate their emotions. Unfortunately, this person isn't really capable of being with someone else in a genuine way. Obviously, this is not the person you want to attract or pursue in a relationship. The best defense against this type of relationship is to be dedicated to self-love and take care of yourself first.

Real love can only happen between people who know how to love and care for *themselves*. Ironically, people who do not practice self-care and try to unconditionally love others cannot get there. While they may believe they can love their partner without conditions, their self-abandonment drains them from being truly emotionally available and healthy. Instead, a person who doesn't take care of themselves is broken. Since they do not know how to care for their own emotions, they are unable to appropriately deal with the needs and emotions of their partner. Conflicts that inevitably arise over time eventually lead to heartbreak.

If you wonder why you keep ending up with "bad boys" or "bad girls," take a look at your level of self-abandonment. The people you are meeting are a reflection of how you feel about yourself. You can remedy this problem and find the relationship you want with someone who better matches your desires when you learn to love and take care of yourself in a better way. *If you want to attract more emotionally available partners who are willing and able to love you in the way you want to be loved, you have to stop pushing aside your feelings, harshly criticizing and judging yourself, and/or using addictive behavior to quiet your emotional needs.*

This is a relatively simple fix, but if you have years of practice abandoning yourself, it may take some time, attention, and effort to undo the damage. Chapter 6 (Tips for Thriving) has some good tips for understanding more about self-love and either beginning the journey or deepening your self-care. You can start by taking responsibility for your feelings. If you are feeling unloved, rejected, or unworthy, you can practice self-love and acceptance to turn that around. Stop looking for a mate to make you feel loved and lovable; make a decision to love and care for yourself first.

Here are some tangible simple examples of taking care of yourself to give you an idea of what is helpful: walk barefoot in the grass, read a book on a blanket in the park, create something (e.g., paint, write a song, build a shelf), take a nap, etc.

*When my divorce ended, I made a commitment to run every day. I am an awful runner, but the commitment to move every day was lifesaving. My latest breakup was in winter, and this time, I chose to walk every day. I used that time to see the beauty around me and listen to healing messages and podcasts. These kinds of activities definitely regenerate. Making it a habit ensured I got a dose of healing whether I felt like it or not. Some days I didn't want to go, but I **never** regretted it afterward.*

When you learn to care for yourself and your emotions, you will coincidentally meet people who know how to take care of themselves. If you take this on and change to a more self-loving approach, you will become less attracted to and may even be repelled by people who are unloving to themselves. Being with someone who knows how to care for themselves means they will know more about how to love you too.

There is an important "watch-out" before tackling self-love that is important to ensure you will be successful: Your intention is important. You need to practice self-care for the right reasons. If you choose to practice self-love solely because you want to attract a better partner, you may have some wins just from being more loving to yourself, but your focus on doing it to attract a mate will actually slow your progress. Remember your brain will pick up on the subtleties of your thinking which can sabotage what you are trying to do. You have to authentically care for yourself. You are so worth it. What do you have to lose?

There is one more point to make regarding self-love and our relationships with our children. As a parent (or someone who wants to be a parent someday), you have a tremendous opportunity to demonstrate and role model a healthy relationship between you and your partner, as well as between you and your children. Most people did not have perfect parents who taught them how to take care of themselves and process their emotions in a healthy way. If this is true for you, you have an opportunity to break this pattern for your children. If today you are not motivated to engage in self-care for yourself, do it for your children. If you already have children, no matter how old they are, it is never too late to start. Even if your children are grown adults living away from home, they can still learn from your example. They will notice the changes in you and may become more open to taking care of themselves.

Getting It Right

- The path to having a great relationship and maintaining it is to become happier and take responsibility for your own happiness.
- No matter what else you do, the most important thing is to pay attention to your thinking.
- Set an intention to enjoy the experience of dating. Dating is not just a means to an end (i.e., finding an ideal partner, getting the relationship).
- Put yourself in the right frame of mind before dating. Expect to have fun, look for the best in your dates, and enjoy the journey. Let go of negative thoughts or feelings about the dating experience, start again with

fresh eyes and hopeful expectations now that you have new tools.

- Look for the best in your potential partners, give them the benefit of the doubt, and remember to avoid the cognitive biases that sabotage your perceptions. If you form a negative impression, you can check out your facts by asking questions or looking for confirmation before locking in your perceptions.

- There are many beliefs that may be influencing your decisions about sex in dating. Your activity may even be based on your beliefs about your partners' beliefs. It's important to understand your beliefs, and challenge and change the ones that don't serve you.

- If you are still struggling to find the relationship you want, there may be subtle beliefs sabotaging you (e.g., myths about relationships, partners, yourself).

- Many people are unaware of the impact of their beliefs, words, and thoughts. If you aren't getting the results you want, you are probably falling prey to your own negative thinking.

- While thinking about a great relationship helps you find one, it can backfire if you are subtly focused on the fact that you don't have the one you want *now*.

- It's important to remember that finding a great partner and a relationship will not make you happy. Your happiness comes from inside of you. You always bring yourself to the party. If you are not happy, no one or relationship can change that for you. Increase your own happiness and then enjoy a fabulous relationship, which will be the icing on the cake.

My Own Next Chapter

I recognize that readers may be curious about my life as the author of this book. While I'm a pretty private person, I thought it might be helpful to know how I've walked the walk regarding the pain of the breakup, the work and the journey of my recovery to my current state of thriving. You've learned bits and pieces of my story throughout the book, but maybe this last part pulls the rest of the story together.

When I got divorced after 33 years of marriage, I assumed I would be alone the rest of my life. I made this assumption because of the horror stories I heard from other divorced women who were my age. They told me that there were no good men out there. They shared miserable dating stories. I saw some friends meet men and then remarry into what seemed like unhappy marriages to me. I knew for a fact that men my age preferred younger women. I had a Ph.D. and a good job, and I understood that professional women were intimidating for men. So, you can understand why I was prepared to be alone. Frankly, I was okay with that. I had a great family, a good job, friends, and many personal interests to pursue. My mindset was "I'll be happy alone and it's time to put me first."

However, to my very great surprise, ten days after my divorce was final, I met an attractive, professional man who liked me, and I liked him. I couldn't have been more astounded. We were in a relationship together for nine months. It was exactly what I needed and was so healing for me. After we broke up, I was alone for about eight months.

I really didn't date too much during that time; instead I used it as a time for learning and growth.

I realized that there was very little time in my life when I was alone. I am the oldest of ten children, so I was always surrounded by people growing up. I didn't go away to college, got married young, and wanted to enjoy some time getting to know myself alone. I began to challenge myself to do things on my own. I went to a comedy club alone, a local bar alone a couple of times, and did some volunteer activities where I didn't know anyone. I was determined to do the things that made me happy whether I had a partner, a friend, or was alone. One night I went to a charity event alone and met a group of people who invited me to the VIP section. It was there that I met my ex. He was my age, very attractive, successful, and we were incredibly compatible. We had what I considered to be a wonderful relationship and a lot of fun over the next two years.

Since we broke up, I focused on finishing a substantial renovation of my condo, learning to live during the COVID-19 pandemic, transitioned out of a 14-year corporate job, started a new business, and wrote this book. I have cultivated amazing friendships with five men who were not in my life before (two of which started with dating) and several girlfriends I've gotten a lot closer to. This was something that was previously missing in my life.

It's been a year of growth, and I am again beginning to think about my next romantic endeavor. I have some intentions about the next relationship, but I honestly don't think much about it because I feel fulfilled and happy with my life today. I'm grateful that I wasn't in a relationship this year because I needed to focus on myself and give myself the time and attention I needed. I know I'll be ready for the next chapter because I am not looking for someone to complete me, take care of me, or make me happy. I can do all of those things for myself. I only want someone to enjoy life with, be the icing on my cake.

I know the success formula for me is to be happy and love myself. I know I am loved by my family and the rich network of friends I have in my life. I am feeling very fulfilled, challenged, and excited about life. Because of this attitude, I know I have an "energy" that is attractive. One of my male friends told me that the women he dates tell him there are not many "evolved" men who are emotionally mature, confident, and healthy. I mentioned how odd it was that I had the opposite experience. Except for one or two cases, I would describe all of the men I met this year as evolved. Is this the self-fulfilling prophecy at work?

Sometimes someone asks me if I'm seeing anyone, and I understand there's a natural curiosity about that, but my preference would be if they ask me if I'm happy. I wonder if we subtly and innocently perpetuate the idea that our lives are incomplete if we are not with a partner?

Here is what I took away from these experiences. In both relationships since my divorce, I've met attractive, fun, successful, smart men who were my age and we had great relationships. I was not focused on finding someone in either case. Instead, I was focused on me and my happiness. As I mentioned above, when I got divorced, I thought I'd be alone, so I didn't have any of those subtle, resistant thoughts around what I was missing. I have no doubt that this pattern of relationships with great men will continue for me. After my last relationship ended, I was not truly happy for a long time. I am grateful because I was challenged to discover a lot about myself and have grown exponentially. I'm back to a place where I am filled with real joy and happiness. I'm not waiting for ANYTHING to make me happy. I can't wait to see what's next.

You can learn more about becoming happier and more optimistic by visiting my website:

www.growoptimism.com

Check out the ReSingled website to find the most current resources, information, or contact me:

www.resingled.net

Questions to Unpack Emotions

To process your emotions, as you are discovering, you must first identify and define them. It is not unusual to struggle with this a bit. If you are unsure of your emotions or need help understanding them, some examples of the typical feelings associated with a breakup are provided below. These questions can help you drill down and more clearly identify what you are feeling.

In this exercise, review the list of typical negative emotions common in a breakup and these questions for each:

1) Were any of these emotions present in your breakup?
2) What was different?
3) What other feelings did you experience during or in the aftermath of your breakup?
4) Which points might still bother you and need further processing?

Anger: Are you angry...?

- At your ex?
  - o How could my partner do this to me?
  - o For what they said, did, or didn't do that led to the end of the relationship (e.g., cheating, ultimatums, alcoholism).
  - o For giving up on the relationship.
  - o For misunderstanding you so maliciously, not giving you the benefit of the doubt.
  - o For how the breakup was communicated (e.g. ghosting, text, publicly, etc.).
  - o Handling the breakup better than you did.

- At yourself?
  - For what you said, did, or didn't do that contributed toward ending the relationship.
  - Your behavior, words, action or inaction that hurt the other person.
  - For letting yourself get hurt.
  - For being stupid, not protecting yourself, not seeing this coming.
  - _____

Sadness/Loss: Are you sad because...

- The relationship is over.
- You lost your best friend.
- You lost your lover.
- You miss being with them.
- You loved them and you can't just stop loving on a dime.
- _____

Insecure: Do you feel insecure because...

- You planned a future together or you hoped to have a future with them.
- You depended on them financially. How will you live?
- You depended on them for everything—you are totally on your own now.
- Nothing is the same.
- You gave the best years and now you are starting over.
- _____

Self-worth: Do you feel...

- Discarded, kicked to the curb.
- Under-appreciated.
- Unlovable.
- _____

Hurt: Do you feel hurt because...

- They moved on so easily. You didn't mean anything to them.
- They stopped talking to you.
- What they said or did hurt you.
- You feel used.
- You feel betrayed.
- _____

Confusion: Do you feel confused because...

- You are not sure about what happened or why.
- You don't know what to do now.
- You don't know if you should reconcile or move on.
- You don't know what you did wrong or what to do so this doesn't happen again.
- _____

Appendix A

Resources:

The resources below (e.g., websites, books, etc.) are provided by chapter. They are not intended to be an exhaustive representation of all the best resources; instead, they are offered to help you get started with topics you may be interested in.

Chapter 6: Tips for Thriving

5 Love Languages – Gary Chapman:
https://www.5lovelanguages.com

Co-dependency:
Co-Dependents Anonymous https://coda.org

https://www.goodtherapy.org/learn-about-therapy/issues/codependency

Kindness Meditation:
https://positivepsychology.com/compassion-meditation/

https://www.contemplativemind.org/practices/tree/loving-kindness

"I found someone"
Song by Blake Shelton
https://www.youtube.com/watch?v=qAc94xiqlNo

Chapter 7: Helpful People

Neuroscience – rewiring the brain:
https://positivepsychology.com/neuroplasticity/

Chapter 9: Making Changes: Beware of Short-Term Gain with Long-Term Pain

Emotional Eating:
https://www.huffpost.com/entry/emotional-eating-triggers_1_5c61c803e4b028d543169e60

https://www.medicinenet.com/emotional_eating/article.htm

Chapter 11: Diffusing Negative Emotions

Emotion Vocabulary Lists:

Pinterest Printable Lists
https://www.google.com/search?sxsrf=ALeKk03k-vqwWdBUnLWC9DtlL59OxM-vDg:1611319381228&source=univ&tbm=isch&q=free+printable+lists+of+emotions+and+definitions&sa=X&ved=2ahUKEwjGvNm6yK_uAhVGGs0KHVZ6BtAQjJkEegQIAxAB&biw=1278&bih=619

Download a List (option for list with Faces or a Customizable Version) https://www.therapistaid.com/therapy-worksheet/list-of-emotions

Plutchiks Model of Emotions
https://www.6seconds.org/2020/08/11/plutchik-wheel-emotions/?gclid=Cj0KCQiAjKqABhDLARIsABbJr Gm6yc8s6m2Y2Oa4-V6MQWWroCSpGhn69ip3WfOB51K53XETV49-eVYaArVlEALw_wcB

300 Emotions (from around the world)
https://designepiclife.com/list-of-emotions/

Cognitive Behavioral Therapy:
https://www.apa.org/ptsd-guideline/patients-and-families/cognitive-behavioral

https://www.psychologytools.com/self-help/what-is-cbt/

Sedona Method:
https://www.sedona.com/Home.asp

Holistic Coaches:
https://anthropedia.org/the-science-of-well-being/

EFT Resources:
https://www.thetappingsolution.com
https://www.eftuniverse.com/eft-workshops-and-training/

https://www.tapwithbrad.com/why-eft/
http://www.energypsych.com/

Energy Practitioners:
https://www.energypsych.org/page/Findpractitioner
https://www.drerinshannon.com/EnergyMedicine.en.html

Energy Medicine:
https://edenmethod.com/essentials-of-energy-medicine/

Emotion Code
https://discoverhealing.com
Practitioners:
https://discoverhealing.com/practitioner-map/

Reiki:
https://www.reiki.org

Meta-analysis:
https://www.meta-analysis.com/pages/why_do.php?cart=

Chapter 14: The Importance of Happiness

Optimism Research Summary and Test:
www.growoptimism.com

Greater Good Science: Science Based Insights for a
Meaningful Life (University of California, Berkley)
https://greatergood.berkeley.edu

Biblical reference to joy:
https://www.christianbiblereference.org/faq_WordC
ount.htm
https://www.openbible.info/topics/joy

Meditation:

Top 25 Best Meditation Resources: Guided
Meditation, Meditation Music, and Meditation Apps
https://www.psycom.net/mental-health-
wellbeing/meditation-resources

34 Free Guided Meditation Resources for Difficult
Times
https://www.mindfullycity.com/free-guided-
meditation-resources-for-difficult-times/

Lyubomirsky, S. (2007). *The how of happiness: A
scientific approach to getting the life you want.*
Penguin Press.

St. John, N. (2014). *Afformations: The miracle of
positive self-talk.* Hay House Inc.

Chapter 16: Putting the Positive Relationship Mindset into Action

Touch Research Institute:
http://pediatrics.med.miami.edu/touch-research/research

References:

Chapter 1: Trauma

1. Kübler-Ross, E. (1970). *On death and dying.* Collier Books/Macmillan Publishing Co.

2. Maslow, A. H. (1954). *Motivation and personality.* Harper and Row.

Chapter 2: Emotions and Your Busy Brain

3. Lerner, J., Li, Y., Valdesolo, P., & Kassas, K. (2015). Emotion and Decision Making. *Annual Review of Psychology, 66:1,* 799-823.

4. Bohn, R. & Short, J. (2012). Measuring Consumer information. *International Journal of Communication 6,* 980–1000.

Chapter 3: Brain Biases

5. Fowler, G. & De Avila, J. (2009). On the internet, everyone's a critic but they're not very critical, *The Wall Street Journal.* [available at https://www.wsj.com/articles/SB125470172872063071].

6. Herr, P. M., Kardes, F. & Kim, J. (1991). Effects of word-of-mouth and product-attribute information on persuasion: An accessibility-diagnosticity perspective. *Journal of Consumer Research, 17(4),* 454-62.

7. Basuroy, S., Chatterjee, S., & Ravid S. (2003). How critical are critical reviews? The box office effects

of film critics, star power, and budgets. *Journal of Marketing, 61 (October)*, 103-117.

8. Chevalier, J. & Mayzlin, D. (2006). The effect of word of mouth on sales: Online book reviews. *Journal of Marketing Research, 43 (August)*, 345-54.

9. Baumeister, R., Bratslavsky, E., Finkenauer,C. & Vohs, K. (2001). Bad is stronger than good. *Review of General Psychology, 5(4)*, 323-70.

10. Understanding the stress response. Harvard Health Publishing. [available at: https://www.health.harvard.edu/staying-healthy/understanding-the-stress-response].

11. McCormick, I. A.; Walkey, F. H.; Green, D. E. (June 1986). Comparative perceptions of driver ability: A confirmation and expansion. *Accident Analysis & Prevention, 18(3)*, 205–208.

Chapter 5: Understanding the Power of Emotions

12. Davis, R.N., & Nolen-Hoeksema, S. (2000). Cognitive inflexibility among ruminators and nonruminators. *Cognitive Therapy & Research, 24*, 699–711. http://dx.doi.org/10.1023/A:1005591412406

13. Lyubomirsky, S., Tucker, K. L., Calwell, N., D, & Berg, K. (1999). Why ruminators are poor problem solvers: Clues from the phenomenology of dysphoric rumination. *Journal of Personality and Social Psychology, 77(5)*, 1041- 1060. http://dx.doi.org/10.1037/0022-3514.77.5.1041

14. Nolen-Hoeksema, S., & Davis, C.G. (1999). ''Thanks for sharing that'': Ruminators and their social support networks. *Journal of Personality and Social Psychology, 77(4)*, 801–814. http://dx.doi.org/10.1037/0022- 3514.77.4.801

15. Fredrickson, B. (2015). Live Q & A with Emiliana Simon-Thomas and Barbara Fredrickson – Week 1. In D. Keltner & E. Simon-Thomas, *The science of happiness.* edX. https://www.edx.org/course/the-science-of-happiness.

16. Gilbert, D. T., Pinel, E. C., Wilson, T. D., Blumberg, S. J., & Wheatley, T. P. (1998). Immune neglect: A source of durability bias in affective forecasting. *Journal of Personality and Social Psychology, 75(3),* 617-638. doi:10.1037/0022-3514.75.3.617

Chapter 6: Tips for Thriving

17. Neff, K. (2011). *Self-Compassion.* William Morrow.

18. Von Soest, T., Kvalem, I., & Wichstrøm, L. (2012). Predictors of cosmetic surgery and its effects on psychological factors and mental health: A population-based follow-up study among Norwegian females. *Psychological Medicine, 42(3),* 617-626. doi:10.1017/S0033291711001267.

19. Jackson, et al., (2014).Psychological changes following weight loss in overweight and obese adults: A prospective cohort study.*PLOS, 9(8):* e104552.

Chapter 7: Helpful People

20. Kahneman, D. (2011) *Thinking fast and slow.* Farrar, Strauss, Giroux.

21. Grim, R., Spring, K., & Dietz, N. (2007). The health benefits of volunteering. A review of recent research. *Corporation for National & Community Service.*

https://www.nationalservice.gov/pdf/07_0506_hbr.pdf

Chapter 9: Making Changes: Beware of Short-Term Gain with Long-Term Pain

22. Mauss, I. (2017). Live Q & A with Emiliana Simon-Thomas and Iris Mauss. In D. Keltner & E. Simon-Thomas, The science of happiness. edX. https://www.edx.org/course/the-science-of-happiness.

23. Simon-Thomas (2017). Live Q & A with Emiliana Simon-Thomas and Iris Mauss. In D. Keltner & E. Simon-Thomas, The science of happiness. edX. https://www.edx.org/course/the-science-of-happiness.

24. Chida, Y. & Steptoe, A. (2009). The association of anger and hostility with future coronary heart disease. A meta-analytic review of prospective evidence. Journal of the American College of Cardiology, 53(11).

25. Bhattacharya, S. (2003). Brain study links negativity emotions and lowered immunity. New Scientist. https://www.newscientist.com/article/dn4116-brain-study-links-negative-emotions-and-lowered-immunity/.

26. Singer, M. A. (2007). The untethered soul: The journey beyond yourself. New Harbinger Publications.

Chapter 11: Diffusing Negative Emotions

27. Clond, M. (2016). Emotional freedom techniques for anxiety: A systematic review with meta-analysis. Journal of Nervous and Mental Disease, 204(5), 388-95. doi: 10.1097/NMD.0000000000000483
28. Sebastian, B., & Nelms, J. (2017). The effectiveness of emotional freedom techniques in the treatment of posttraumatic stress disorder: A meta-analysis. Explore: The Journal of Science and Healing, 13(1), 16-25. http://dx.doi.org/10.1016/j.explore.2016.10.001
29. Mavranezouli I., Megnin-Viggars O., Daly C., et al (2020). Research review: psychological and psychosocial treatments for children and young people with posttraumatic stress disorder: a network meta-analysis. J Child Psychol Psychiatry 61:18–29. https://doi.org/10.1111/jcpp.13094

Chapter 13: Science of Beliefs

30. Sharma, N. & Sharma, K. (2015). Self-Fulfilling Prophecy: A Literature Review. International Journal of Interdisciplinary and Multidisciplinary Studies, 2(3), 41- 52.
31. Rosenthal, R., & Babad, E. Y. (1985). Pygmalion in the gymnasium. Educational Leadership, 43(1), 36–39.
32. Rosenthal, R., & Jacobson, L. (1968). Pygmalion in the classroom. Urban Rev 3, 16–20. https://doi.org/10.1007/BF02322211
33. Aaronson, L. (2005). Self-fulfilling prophecies: Expectations of stereotypes will come to pass if people believe in them. Psychology Today.

https://www.psychologytoday.com/us/articles/2005 03/self-fulfilling-prophecies

34. Jussim, L. & Eccles, J. (1995). Naturalistic studies of interpersonal expectancies. Review of Personality and Social Psychology 15:74–108.

35. Jussim, L. (1991). Social perception and social reality: A reflection-construction model. Psychological Review 98:54–73.

36. McNulty, S. E., & Swann, W. B., Jr. (1994). Identity negotiation in roommate relationships: The self as architect and consequence of social reality. Journal of Personality and Social Psychology, 67(6), 1012–1023.

37. Downey, G., Freitas, A. Bichaelis, B., & Khouri, H (1998). The self-fulfilling prophecy in close relationships: Rejection sensitivity and rejection by romantic partners. Journal of Personality and Social Psychology, 75(2), 545-560.

38. Biggs, M. (2009). Self-fulfilling prophecies. In P. Bearman & P. Hedström (Eds.) The Oxford handbook of analytical sociology (pp. 294-314). Oxford University Press.

Chapter 14 The Importance of Happiness

39. Böhm,R., Schütz, A., Rentzsch, K., Körner, A. & Funke, F. (2010). Are we looking for positivity or similarity in a partner's outlook on life? Similarity predicts perceptions of social attractiveness and relationship quality. The Journal of Positive Psychology,5(6),431-438, DOI: 10.1080/17439760.2010.534105

40. Coyne, J. C. (1976). Depression and the response of others. Journal of Abnormal Psychology, 85(2), 186–193. https:// https://doi.org/10.1037/0021-843X.85.2.

41. General Social Survey: https://gssdataexplorer.norc.org/trends/Gender%20 &%20Marriage?measure=happy
42. Lucas et al. (2003). Reexamining adaptation and the Set Point Model of Happiness: Reactions to changes in marital status. *Journal of Personality and Social Psychology, 84(3)*, 527-539.
43. Achor, S. (2010). *The Happiness Advantage: The seven principles of positive psychology that fuel success and performance at work.* Crown Business/Random House.
44. Lyubomirsky S., King, L., & Diener, E. (2005). The benefits of frequent positive affect: Does happiness lead to success? *Psychological Bulletin, 131(6)*, 803–855. DOI: 10.1037/0033-2909.131.6.803.
45. Simon-Thomas, (2020). Specific Benefits to Happiness. In D. Keltner & E. Simon-Thomas, *The science of happiness.* edX. https://www.edx.org/course/the-science-of-happiness.
46. Lyubomirsky, S.(2007). *The how of happiness: A scientific approach to getting the life you want.* Penguin Press.

Chapter 15: Increasing Happiness

47. Kahneman, D. & Deaton, A. (2010). High income improves evaluation of life but not emotional well-being. *PNAS, 107(38)*, 16489-16493.
48. Boven, L., & Gilovich, T. (2003). To do or to have? that is the question. *Journal of Personality and Social Psychology, 85(6)*, 1193–1202.
49. Kumar A., Killingsworth, M.A., & Gilovich T. (2014). Waiting for merlot: Anticipatory

consumption of experiential and material purchases. *Psychological Science, 25(10)*, 1924-31. doi: 10.1177/0956797614546556.

50. Fredrickson, B. (2015). Live Q & A with Emiliana Simon-Thomas and Barbara Fredrickson. In D. Keltner & E. Simon-Thomas, *The science of happiness*. edX. https://www.edx.org/course/the-science-of-happiness.

51. Otake, K., Shimai, S., Tanaka-Matsumi, J., Otsui, K., & Fredrickson, B. L. (2006). Happy people become happier through kindness: A counting kindnesses intervention. *Journal of happiness studies, 7*(3), 361–375. https://doi.org/10.1007/s10902-005-3650-z

52. Teasdale, J.D., Segal, Z.V., Williams J., Ridgeway V.A., Soulsby, J.M., & Lau, M.A. (2000). Prevention of relapse/recurrence in major depression by mindfulness-based cognitive therapy. *Journal of Consulting and Clinical Psychology 68(4)*, 615–623.

53. Music and Health (2011). *Harvard Health Publishing*. https://www.health.harvard.edu/staying-healthy/music-and-health

Chapter 16: Putting the Positive Relationship Mindset into Action

54. Keltner, D. (2020).Dacher Keltner on Touch. In D. Keltner & E. Simon-Thomas, *The science of happiness*. edX. https://www.edx.org/course/the-science-of-happiness.

55. Lucas et al. (2003). Reexamining Adaptation and the Set Point Model of Happiness: Reactions to Changes in Marital Status. *Journal of Personality and Social Psychology, 84(3)*, 527-539.

56. Geers, A.L., Reilley, S.P., Dember, W.N., (1998). Optimism, pessimism, and friendship. Current Psychology, 17, 3–19.
57. Srivastava, S., McGonigal, K.M., Richards, J.M., Butler, E.A., & Gross, J.J. (2006). Optimism in close relationships: How seeing things in a positive light makes them so. *Journal of Personality and Social Psychology, 91(1),*143-53. doi: 10.1037/0022-3514.91.1.143. PMID: 16834485.
58. Assad, K. K., Donnelan, B. M., & Conger, R. D. (2007). Optimism: An enduring resource for romantic relationships. *Journal of Personality and Social Psychology, 93,* 285–297.
59. Campbell, K., Nelson, J., Parker, M. L., & Johnston, S. (2018). Interpersonal chemistry in friendships and romantic relationships. *Interpersona: An International Journal on Personal Relationships, 12(1),* 34-50. doi:10.5964/ijpr.v12i1.289.

References

About the Author

Laura Heft, Ph.D. is Behavioral Scientist, Optimism expert, Psychologist, and author dedicated to helping people become more optimistic and successful. Understanding that people are surprisingly unaware of why they do what they do and what influences their decisions, Laura is committed to leveraging the power of science to improve their lives.

After a personally tough breakup, she decided to apply what she knew about behavioral science (the head) and emotions (the heart) to help get through her own challenges and *thrive*. As she shared what she learned with friends and family, she realized others would benefit from the same behavioral science tools and awareness to recover from breakups faster and get the relationships they wanted.

Laura has over 20 years of experience in Fortune 500 companies as a coach and consultant on behavioral science, motivation, leadership, and employee and organization development. She is the founder and CEO of GrowOptimism LLC, a company that delivers science-based solutions that drive higher performance through consulting, training, and coaching, including an assessment that not only identifies a person's level of optimism but also provides feedback on strengths and opportunities.

You can contact her at www.growoptimism.com.

Made in the USA
Middletown, DE
02 December 2021

54054890R00179